HEARTFELT HOMEBAKED WISDOM

Simple Practices for a Meaningful Life

Maree Allan Fowler

HEARTFELT HOMEBAKED WISDOM

Author: Maree Allan Fowler
Editors: Anna Featherstone, Georgia Spanos
Cover Design: Valeriia T
Character Design: Alice Fowler
Character Illustrations & Book Formatting: Cindy Lee

We acknowledge the Traditional Owners of the land where this book was written, the Wurrundjeri, Kulin and Wulgurukaba Nations, and pay respects to their Elders past and present.

A catalogue record for this book is available from the National Library of Australia

ISBN-13: 978-1-7642252-0-5

First Published 2026

This book is dedicated to my spiritual teachers - Lama Marut and Cindy Lee, Pippa Loveday and Shadi Mogadime. And of course, many others too, including dear friends and family. I love and appreciate you all with all my heart. You have generously taught me, allowing me to remember, access, understand and integrate this truth or wisdom, so that it truly becomes heartfelt as a way to live my life with contentment and meaning.

TABLE OF CONTENTS

WELCOME ~ Pg. 1

1. GRATITUDE ~ Pg. 8

2. GIVING & RECEIVING ~ Pg. 46

3. FOUNDATIONAL PRACTICES ~ Pg. 71

A Toolkit to a Happier Life

4. CAUSALITY/KARMA ~ Pg. 104

And The First Three of the Ten Guidelines

5. TEN GUIDELINES FOR A GOOD LIFE ~ Pg. 132

The Seven Related to Speech and Mind

6. DEFRAZZLING ~ Pg. 160

Coming Back to the Present

7. FOSTERING COMPASSION & PEACE OF MIND ~ Pg. 186

8. UNDERSTANDING FORGIVENESS ~ Pg. 210

9. KINDNESS TO ALL (INCLUDING OURSELVES) ~ Pg. 254

EPILOGUE ~ Pg. 285 | APPENDIX ~ Pg. 287

WELCOME

Dear Reader,

Thank you for giving me this opportunity to share my, heartfelt, home-baked wisdom with you. Wisdom that has truly come from the heart through connecting with my spiritual teachers, most especially Lama Marut and Cindy Lee. Putting it into practice in my daily life is the 'home-baked' nature of things.

These days, I like to believe that the movie of my life is happening *for* me, rather than to me. And that I have a wise internal director guiding me in every role and scene I play. I call this director my 'wise self', though you may prefer another name such as your Soul, True Nature, Buddha Nature, Love, God, Good, Internal Guru, or Universal Wisdom.

Like you, I've played, and continue to play, many changing roles in life: daughter, sister, partner, colleague and mother. And like you, I play these roles in different settings in everyday life—at work, at home, in the community or on holiday.

I haven't always been a skilled actor in these roles though! Which is why I'm grateful to have received some very wise 'acting advice' from my spiritual teachers. This guidance has gifted me wonderful tools and tips greatly improving my ability to 'perform' with more wisdom and heart—and included in this book for you are many of my favourites.

These handed-down ancient wisdoms from many sources offer us tools to live our everyday lives with contentment, purpose, peace of mind and benefit to others. They also remind us of the inner wisdom we all possess: the internal director, a knowing truth within the heart, which is available any time. We just need to learn to listen. We all have this internal wise director. Yes, you too! It's a wisdom that is truly heartfelt.

I guess that I've always had a sense that there's more to me than my physical human form. I can remember having the first little inkling of this as a four- or five-year-old. Things were tricky at home, and I was lying in bed trying to get to sleep. I felt sad, alone and scared—but I also sensed a loving presence within and felt held, reassured and comforted.

I realise now this little spark of knowing has always been with me. And while it's always present, it's often not accessed due to the chaos of growing up, having a career, family life and all that comes with it. My little wise self director spark was reignited though through my interest in spirituality. I see now that this inner director is kind, encouraging, compassionate, always available when I need direction and loves me unconditionally—warts and all.

As I mentioned, I don't always remember to tune in and listen to what my wise director directs, especially during difficult scenes. Sometimes my task master ego director is so loud that I don't even hear the quiet truth of the wiser one.

Sometimes I find it hard to remember that life is happening *for* me, and that my wise director really does have my best interests at heart—even when I'm cast in the tougher scenes. Those scenes include when someone I love (human or furry) is sick or dying, when I lose a job, face health problems, or feel overwhelmed by the conflict and tragedy in the world.

When I truly believe that life is happening *for* me and that my internal wise director is managing these scenes as opportunities for learning and finding meaning, then I can stop being a victim of life and events, and instead take responsibility to act, speak and think in the wise ways I am being guided.

That's not to say it's easy! It requires radical acceptance—what Lama Marut would call 'it is like this now'—instead of a protest that somehow things should be different from how they actually are. It requires willingness and courage to meet our experiences, process and release them, and make space for love, compassion, wisdom and meaning.

The home-baked quality of the wisdom in this book refers to my efforts to put the tools and wise acting advice into practice in my everyday life and to tune in to my wise director, in the many roles I play. Through trying things out, or practicing in my test kitchen, I have found that this wisdom integrates into who I am. There is certainly proof (and truth) in the pudding!

It's more than ten years since I began studying spirituality, including Tibetan Buddhism and yoga. It all began when I received a book voucher for managing my boys' basketball team. I was drawn to the Spirituality section of the book shop and chose Sarah Napthali's 'Buddhism For Mothers'.[1] This lead me on quest to find a local teacher and group and eventually, a seemingly random but life-changing connection with Lama Marut and Cindy Lee. These teachers and teachings radically changed my life for the better. My mother saw the early changes in me, making the comment, 'I'm not sure what Maree is up to, but she seems much happier'.

Studying with my teachers has given me many wonderful opportunities. Over the years, I've attended and helped organise teachings and retreats with Lama Marut and Cindy Lee and have also had the opportunity to teach philosophy and yoga.

Most importantly, I've been generously given the tools to live a good, happy life of meaning.

I feel passionate about sharing what I have learnt and practiced, and have done so for many years in a blog that I share through the POM-Melbourne (Peace of Mind – Melbourne) fortnightly newsletter. POM-Melbourne is a cottage industry that raises funds for community projects both in Australia and overseas. We are a small band of volunteers who have fun generating money through yoga classes and the sale of homemade craft, art and baked goods. A percentage of profits from the sale of this book will be donated to POM-Melbourne.

This book is a structured and organised collection of some of those blogs and reflections. They tell of the ways I have done my best to practice and work with the many tools I've been given as I continue to skip and trip along the spiritual path, home baking and integrating this heartfelt wisdom.

Writing Home-Baked, Heartfelt Wisdom has itself been a wonderful 'skipping and tripping' experience. It has helped me learn so much about myself and to face fears, doubts and insecurities. Despite the difficulties and many times, I wanted to quit my wise internal self kept encouraging me to keep going—to do my best to share what I am extremely grateful to have received.

It is my heartfelt wish that these reflections and exercises will help you to live a happier, more meaningful life and remind you to tap into your own internal wisdom.

With love,
Maree

HOW TO USE THIS BOOK

It may be helpful to think of the many ideas and practical applications in this book as a starter toolkit. As you go along, you might pick up a few favourites and even add some of your own.

Trying to master everything at once may feel overwhelming, so there's no need to do that. Instead choose from your little toolkit the tool you need most at any given moment. You might choose to work with one practice for a while, or simply open the book at random and read a page that captures your eye.

There are activity suggestions and contemplations included at the end of each section. You may like to give these suggestions a go, and add them to your personal toolkit.

Please remember to always be kind and encouraging to yourself, especially when you are new to using a tool to create a new helpful habit. And have fun playing around with new ideas, it's how we learn and grow!

1. GRATITUDE

GRATITUDE

I truly believe gratitude is one of the most important foundational practices for happiness, so it seems the ideal place to begin this book. It's a superpower really—scientifically proven to boost our joy, peace of mind, well-being and confidence. The realisation we can choose gratitude to cultivate happiness, abundance and optimism is life changing. Outlined in this section are some benefits of being grateful; the 'Two-Part Morning Loll'—a morning gratitude and impermanence contemplation; reflections on gratitude for motherly kindness, ourselves and others. Thank you for taking the time to contemplate and practice gratitude, and here's to the happiness it brings into your life.

Gratitude, Our Superpower

Let's explore the transformative power of gratitude and its profound impact on wellbeing, confidence and happiness.

I chuckled recently when I saw the warning label message on a pillbox. It read: 'Gratitude may cause shifts in perspective (most certainly in the positive direction!), may cause feelings of joy and abundance and decreased fear and anxiety.'

That's why gratitude is a pill I'm happy to not only swallow but chew on too! It's one of the most important foundational practices for happiness, resilience, confidence, peace of mind and feelings of abundance. It can also help us overcome feelings of sadness, hopelessness, fear, anxiety and the destructive force of taking things for granted and slipping into negative thought patterns.

Gratitude can be defined as *a readiness to show appreciation for and to return kindness.*

It's a human superpower; research proves it and so does evidence from our daily lives. For me, when I remember to be grateful, there's so much more joy in my life and less room for stress.

And there's so much to be grateful for, especially when we acknowledge how much others do for us each day. We all exist in mutual dependence or interdependence, surviving and thriving due to the kindness, care and labour of others. These 'others' may be known, unknown or unseen; but when we notice these contributions it extends our sense of gratitude toward countless beings.

When you think like this, that humble cup of coffee we enjoy suddenly seems not so humble after all! I for one had rarely stopped to think about all the contributors to my daily brew—those who grew the beans, harvested, processed, packed and shipped them. There's also the barista making the magic, the café owner, and so on. Everything exists in this interdependent network so when we stop to consider all the people at play making our lives possible, it's hard *not* to feel grateful.

Expressing that gratitude is essential for our well-being and for nurturing meaningful connection. Acknowledging the kindness and care we receive—from family, friends and colleagues—strengthens those relationships and supports our own happiness. Extending that appreciation to strangers who show us everyday kindness also cultivates peace and positivity.

It may seem like a strange approach, but we can also be thankful for the people and beings who *give* us opportunities to practise kindness. Without our friends, family, children, pets, and even strangers, we wouldn't have as many chances to grow our love, compassion, generosity, and understanding. We can also direct gratitude inward, recognising the kindness we offer others and becoming our own encouraging cheer squad.

And when things go wrong, remembering to forgive ourselves and others, and to view challenges as learning opportunities, helps us stay grounded in gratitude even during life's inevitable mishaps.

It's fun too to realise that when we're kind and thankful to ourselves and others, we create a more positive self-perception that in turn further boosts our happiness and confidence. Being and seeing ourselves as a force for good in the world actually creates more good forces!

When I was learning about gratitude, it was pointed out that our minds simply cannot be grateful and unhappy at the same time. Focusing on gratitude rather than negativity is now a conscious choice I try to make. It doesn't always come naturally though, which is what we'll explore in the next chapter.

On Choosing Grumpy or Grateful

Ever wake up feeling bleak and blah? I regularly did, until a simple practice transformed my mindset. I learnt that a morning gratitude practice can change everything.

Do you ever start the day irritable, stressed, or with a sense of gloom and doom about the hours ahead? One Sunday morning recently, I woke up feeling exactly this way, and it reminded me of how, years ago, I'd been in the habit of waking up like this regularly. Back then, I was working across town, and each morning I'd hop aboard the 'grumpy negative thought train' with complaints like, 'Oh no, I don't want to get up, I've got to drive to work in all that traffic, I have so many people to see and reports to write, and it's raining!'

Instead of seeing the many positives in my amazing life, I was choosing to focus on what I considered the negatives. At the time, it didn't occur to me that I had a choice! I also didn't realise how unhappy my choice to keep boarding the grumpy train made me.

Fortunately, many years ago I received some wise advice from Lama Marut as to how I could be the driver of my own attitudes, rather than a passenger. It's a very simple mindfulness meditation focusing on gratitude upon waking.

This is now a well-established helpful habit of mine... except for when I occasionally forget, like I did on that recent Sunday.

I'd woken up with a heavy feeling of discontent, focused on what was going wrong (lack of sleep; mechanical problems with our campervan that would delay our 30th wedding anniversary camping trip; a necessary route change that would throw other scrupulously planned plans out). I was toot toot tooting on the grumpy train.

And then, with the tools I'd been given through the Morning Gratitude Practice (shared in the next chapter), I chose to jump off that train.

There was, of course, so much to be grateful for. I had woken up for a start! There was a marriage of 30 years and a beautiful family to be celebrated (what a wonderful assignment from the cosmos)! Let alone, we actually *own* a campervan! I rose feeling much more positive, ready to embrace whatever the weekend's adventure looked like.

We ended up in a beautiful spot in the Grampians in Victoria, the vista reminding me to open up my lens on life instead of narrowing the focus down to the small stuff. I felt so grateful for 30 years of fun, frustration, laughter, love, tears, and joy and the wonderful family and friends with whom I share my life, with all its ups, downs, and interesting twists and turns.

I remembered too having once seen a woman wearing a T-shirt that read, 'Too blessed to be stressed'. It was a good reminder of how blessed I am, and to be grateful for all the wonderful people and things in my life.

Choosing gratitude changes everything so next up is the simple morning gratitude practice that has transformed my grumpy morning mindset habit into a grateful one.

Permission to Loll! A Morning Gratitude Practice

Introducing Lama Marut's 'Two-Part Morning Loll' which in Part One uses gratitude to transform mornings, and thereby our happiness, resilience and peace of mind.

Many years ago, Lama Marut introduced me to a morning gratitude practice which he called the 'Two Part Morning Loll'. Gratitude is the first part of the loll and I remain thankful for it to this day. It's a wonderful way to start each morning as it sets such a positive mood for the day.

In the Loll, he recommends that on waking we don't get up straight away, but that we take some time to loll around in bed feeling grateful. I couldn't help but LOL when I first heard about the Loll, questioning how extended relaxation in bed could possibly better my life. But this restful pleasure—even though the habit takes consistent practice to form—has changed me (for the better, of course!).

Morning Loll Part One:

Lolling in bed (not scrolling in bed!) helps me realise all the little and large things I can be grateful for. You may like to focus on other things, but I find it useful to bring to mind:

> **The kindness and efforts of others in the present:** It's extraordinary how many people, mostly unknown to us, make our lives possible. Farmers grow our food; others harvest, process, pack and transport it. Still more craft the everyday things such as clothes and furniture

that bring us comfort and ease on a daily basis. Others provide services like roads, water, electricity, education and healthcare. As just one example, each morning as I loll I express appreciation for what I'll enjoy at breakfast. I try to remember to be thankful to all those who contribute to what's on my plate—including even the maker of the plate, as well as our chickens Mabel and Myrtle for their 'eggcellent' contributions.

The people of the past: I especially enjoy thinking about the people from the past whose efforts and discoveries have paved the way for our lives today. From creators of delicious recipes to electricity, medical discoveries to the craft of crochet, and inventors of everything from recorded music to prescription glasses. It's hard not to be awed and grateful when you think about it!

The circumstances we were born into: Some of what supports us isn't created by any one person, but comes from conditions we inherit: living in a safe country with abundant resources, having access to clean water and services, and the freedom to build a meaningful life.

Friends, family, and loved ones: We would be nothing without these support systems.

Nature: We have so many wonders to enjoy: spectacular bush, parks, rivers, beaches, and gardens, and all the flora and fauna that live within, under, and above them.

Ourselves: Remembering to be grateful for ourselves, and all the ways in which we are a positive force in the world.

Lolling around in bed and recalling all we can be thankful for reminds us that gratitude can be a way of life.

All Day Gratitude:

Given that gratitude can boost our happiness, there's no need to restrict it to just mornings! Reflecting on what we're grateful for can become an ongoing habit, building on itself so it gradually becomes our natural way of being in and moving through life.

You can get creative with how you cultivate this habit. For instance, keep a gratitude journal and jot things down during the day, or draw something in the evening. Seeing what we're grateful for in visual or written form can help us absorb its meaning more deeply.

To double down on creative gratitude, I love embroidering slogans on tea towels, hankies, and t-shirts!

One Christmas, I made 'Feeling Grateful' pyjamas for Peace of Mind - Melbourne (POM) my cottage industry that raises funds for community projects in Australia and overseas. I came up with the idea to sew the shorts out of old business shirts and the tops out of t-shirt material and then my friend Hilary kindly embroidered the top with the words 'Feeling Grateful'. I still have my pair, and they serve as a great visual reminder to pause and be appreciative.

Practicing gratitude has inspired me to say 'thank you' more often too. I'm always surprised and delighted by the response from people when I genuinely take the time to thank them for a service or kindness. Gratitude connects us all in so many wonderful ways and being generous with our thank-you's is one way to one way to strengthen those connections and brighten everyday moments.

And speaking of bright, why is it that grateful people positively beam?

Find out in the following chapter.

Maybe you would like to embroider your own PJ t-shirt with 'Feeling Grateful' – a beautiful reminder to yourself and others.

Why Do Grateful People Seem So Happy?

Embracing an attitude of gratitude leads to greater health, happiness and resilience in daily life. It's an ongoing effort, but finding even a touch of gratitude every day helps build the habit.

What comes first, the chicken or the egg? Giving or receiving? Contentment or discontentment?

I'll offer the answer as it was once offered to me: contentment is the cure for discontent. Gratitude, it turns out, is the gateway, the key to happiness in our everyday lives. Why? Because when we're grateful for our lives, we're less likely to be unhappy due to constantly wanting more or wishing things to be different.

Our thoughts shape our experience, which is why focusing on what's going wrong or what's lacking often leaves us feeling discontented. Whereas if we want to feel content, abundant, happy, and optimistic, we need to choose to focus our attention on:

- the positive instead of the negative,
- on what is going *right* instead of what is going *wrong*,
- and on what we *have* instead of what we *lack*.

Many studies confirm what we already sense: grateful people are happier people. Neuroscience, through the study of neuroplasticity (the plastic and changeable nature of our brain and mind), has shown that when we choose to be positive and grateful, we strengthen the neural pathways that promote health, happiness and wellbeing.

Not only does practicing gratitude benefit our health, it also:

- gives us an instant boost in happiness, a feeling of optimism and a positive future outlook
- brings us peace of mind and the ability to overcome the tendency to blame and criticise ourselves and others
- helps us understand that our greatest challenges often bring us our greatest lessons and opportunities to grow, which in turn builds our resilience.

Interestingly, gratitude isn't dependent on our circumstances; it's an attitude we can choose, no matter what we're going through.

As English philosopher Francis Bacon reminds us:

> *'It is not happy people who are grateful,*
> *it is grateful people who are happy.'* [2]

There are plenty of good reasons to embrace the attitude of gratitude, but day-to-day life can throw up all sorts of roadblocks to us doing so. Let's navigate those next.

Gratitude: Lost and Found

Often, we become so focussed on what we think we are entitled to or think we deserve; we are unable to see what we already have. Gratitude can uplift, enabling us to find the blessings in difficult situations, enabling us to transform so-called problems into opportunities.

Despite knowing the proven benefits of being grateful, I sometimes forget how destructive it can be to take things for granted. I can also slip into feeling I'm entitled to things being a certain way. When I do that and so-called 'problems' come along (especially the bigger ones!), it can be extremely challenging for me to harness gratitude as a way to uplift myself or uncover the hidden treasure in an experience.

I've learned, though, that turning a problem into an opportunity can be done with time and practice. One way I've built my transformation muscles is by starting with smaller moments.

For example, I can be grateful for the grumpy person ahead of me in the coffee queue for reminding me to be patient. I can be grateful for a traffic jam for giving me the opportunity to slow down, relax and listen to music. And remembering that 'thank you' is one of the most powerful expressions I can offer—both to others and to myself—makes a real difference for me.

A weekend away with friends gave me some unexpected gratitude insights too. While walking along the Queenscliff coastline in Victoria, it began raining, and suddenly I was drenching myself with negative thoughts. 'It *should* be warm and sunny,' I grumbled internally. I became so fixated on what I thought was going wrong that I completely overlooked the breathtaking coastline around me—forgetting to appreciate everything that was going right.

Then Pema Chödrön's advice from *When Things Fall Apart* sprang to mind: 'Appreciate everything, even the ordinary, especially the ordinary.' [3]

Rather than then giving myself a hard time for being negative or ungrateful, I gently reminded myself to tune in: to notice and appreciate the so-called ordinary (AKA extraordinary) place I found myself in. Taking a deep breath, I paused, appreciating the surrounding beauty—the deep grey sky, the soaring birds, the powerful sea, the cool of the raindrops. Soon I pulsed with a genuine sense of gratitude and gladness. A light had turned on inside me.

Like the two lighthouses on the Queenscliff coast, gratitude helps guide where we place our attention. In the next chapter, we'll explore the concept of a Gratitude Spotlight.

Spotlighting the Good We See

The essence of gratitude is a symphony of appreciation and kindness, guiding us toward deeper compassion, forgiveness, and a more connected, joyful life.

One way to bring gratitude into clearer focus is to choose a 'Gratitude Spotlight' for the week. It's not about lighting up everything at once but choosing where to aim the beam.

For example, we can quietly select someone to consciously appreciate, placing them in our internal 'spotlight' and focusing on what they do for us, for others, or for the world. This can inspire us to be more like them or encourage us to express our appreciation through words, actions, or a gift.

Gratitude for a spotlighted person (or people) can be simple and fun when it's someone we admire or find easy to appreciate. But we might also choose to ramp up our spotlight practice to include someone we find challenging to appreciate, perhaps someone who has hurt us. For these more difficult spotlights, I find it helpful to be compassionate and remember that we don't know the deep pain, hurt, or abandonment others have experienced, which may have led them to behave in hurtful ways.

That said, it's important not to trivialise or bypass hurtful experiences and their associated emotions. Forgiveness and compassion are practices in themselves and may take time, patience and support such as through therapy to achieve. (We'll explore this more in the 'Understanding Forgiveness' section, beginning on page 20.)

In my life, I've noticed how easy it is to slip into judgment, negativity, or resentment over how I think my parents 'should have been'. I've caught myself replaying old, unhelpful soundtracks on repeat, but choosing gratitude over resentment has been much more beneficial for me and brought positivity and peace to my life. Through the spotlight process I can easily see there is plenty to be grateful to my parents for—my life for one!

When I shine the Gratitude Spotlight on my parents, I appreciate the amazing life they gave me—their care, teaching, love, and sacrifices; their many sleepless nights; the clothes sewn by hand; meals cooked; washing and ironing done; and the educational opportunities they made possible. I'm also grateful for the ethics and values they taught me and—as they grew older and required care—the opportunities they gave me to develop more tenderness, patience, humility, forgiveness, and compassion.

Before my parents died, my gratitude practice included writing about them in my journal and remembering to thank them personally whenever I could. I also reflected on how I might return their kindness. As they aged and their health, mobility, and independence declined, I had many opportunities to repay them with care and presence.

Sometimes it's beneficial to turn the spotlight on ourselves too, which we'll talk through next.

Gone Fishing: for Gratitude

Discover how to dim the need to fish for compliments.

Opportunities to extend kindness don't always show up in the ways we expect—and often don't result in thanks from others. For example, though I'm grateful for the many opportunities to extend kindness to others, especially in my role as a mother, sometimes such opportunities can be challenging. Most mothers will understand, things like last-minute requests to be driven to school because of a missed bus, or when family meals that take time and effort to prepare are poorly received with 'Oh yuck, not that again'.

Thanking myself during these tricky times prevents me from fishing for or manipulating thanks and becoming resentful—unhelpful mindsets I've been practicing to change. That said, it's preferable to encourage thanks from others, rather than demand or expect it. Thanking myself also helps me become more courageous and confident in doing what I know is most helpful.

As a parent, my kindness has at times taken the form of strong boundaries—which, unsurprisingly, I'm certainly not thanked for in the moment. My boundary statements include classics like, 'Please don't speak to me like that' or 'No, you can't do that.' These firm-but-kind responses come from the wish to protect, guide and avoid harm, but they're often met with stiff resistance—especially from teenagers!

I recall the need for such a strong-yet-kind boundary when I enforced the '*No sleeping with your phone*' rule for my then thirteen-year-old. Discovering the phone hidden under the bedclothes, I removed it—despite animated protests. Checking in with my wiser self, I remembered my intention: to prevent harm and ensure a good night's sleep. I thanked myself for being courageously kind, even as the protests continued (loudly!).

Extending those two powerful words, 'thank you' to all—including myself—has helped me live with more gratitude. It has made me happier, more confident, and more optimistic, and I no longer feel the need to fish for validation from others.

It's surprisingly uplifting to thank your past self too, and we discuss how to do that next.

Thanks, Past Me

The delight in thanking yourself! Try exploring the art of appreciating the efforts made by your past self, which can in turn bring happiness to your present-day.

I was struck by the joy and importance of thanking our past selves when a younger friend of mine, Mary, returned from a holiday and exclaimed, 'I was so grateful to my past self for leaving my room tidy before I went to Japan. It was so nice to come home to a tidy room.'

We're often quite good at expressing thanks to others, but regularly overlook ourselves. This lesson hit home one morning when I happily found the dishwasher empty. I thanked family members, only to discover none of them had done it—then I remembered, it was *me*! I'd emptied it in a sleepy haze before going to bed.

Gratitude flowed toward my past self, who had spared my present self the task by pre-emptively emptying the dishwasher.

I continue to have fun with this practice. After an active weekend—*active*, as my friend Monique kindly reminds me to say, rather than *busy*, because it's more positive and better for peace of mind—I had relatives coming for lunch on Monday and no time for cooking. Opening the freezer, I felt a wave of gratitude for my past self, who had thoughtfully cooked extra food and tucked it away. As I fished out all sorts of goodies—like quiche and sausage rolls—for lunch, I couldn't help but grin and say, 'Thanks, past me!'

There are so many occasions we can practice this, often for things we did in the past that are quietly helping us today. Perhaps it's an email already sent, a bill paid, a course that's led to new insights or a kind decision you once made that's still rippling forward. In thanking our past selves, we're supporting our present lives too. And some of our other biggest supporters are often the mothers of this world and we'll look at how so in the next chapter.

Gratitude For the Motherly

In expanding the concept of motherhood, we see we're all creators in some way—capable of showing 'motherly' care to ourselves and others through kindness, support and compassion.

One May as Mother's Day approached, I found myself exploring what it means to be a mother or motherly toward others. We all know the traditional definition of mother as a 'female parent', but I wanted to expand this understanding. Besides the expected definition, I discovered in the *Oxford English Dictionary* [4] that *mother* can mean 'a condition that gives rise to something else'. This was interesting, as we are constantly creating causes that give rise to other things every time we speak, act, and think. Causality, or karma, is always at play. As Mother Teresa said, 'Kind words can be short and easy to speak, but their echoes are truly endless.' [5] I then looked up synonyms for 'motherly' and found words including affectionate, kind, loving, maternal, and tender.

So, as we are all mothers in the creator sense, it's helpful to be aware of what we are creating with our language, actions, and thoughts. We all have the opportunity to be 'motherly creators' by showing kindness to others, regardless of if we're related. Whether we are a female parent or not, we can be motherly or kind toward children, partners, relatives, friends, strangers, pets, other creatures, the environment and, of course, toward ourselves too.

I enjoy thinking about people who inspire us by showing motherly love toward others. People like Mother Teresa, the Dalai Lama, our friends who are amazing foster parents, a kind truckie who got us out of trouble on a road trip, my Aunt Rosa—who did not have biological children but was so loving toward all her nieces and nephews—and other friends and family, many of whom are also not mothers in the traditional sense.

Though Mother's Day provides a wonderful opportunity to reflect on and be grateful for all mother figures, some of us may have had difficult parenting or family situations. Author and theologian Meggan Watterson, in her book *Mary Magdalene Revealed*, reminds us: 'Even if you have never experienced a mother's love, the genuine force of that loving protection exists within us. So, we can give it to ourselves.' [6] By tuning into our wise self, we can recognise that this love and protection exists within us, allowing us to nurture and give ourselves the love and mothering we need.

A helpful reminder when it comes to a difficult mothering experience is forgiveness. It is never helpful to hold on to past hurts. When we do, we cannot move forward, and through blame, we remain a victim to that particular person or event. Letting the past hurt go allows us to make peace. Forgiveness and letting go does not mean we forget or excuse the hurtful behaviour; it simply means we are no longer willing to relive the particular hurt again and again.

When we choose to let go of past difficulties (and we may need to make that choice again and again), we can begin to reclaim our peace of mind. In these moments, being motherly toward ourselves with kindness, comfort and care, can ease us through the challenges.

And our experiences on this planet are challenging, and it's often hard to feel grateful, especially about loss and grief. That's why the next few chapters are extra useful.

Finding Gratitude Through Life and Loss

Here we contemplate impermanence by learning to practice 'death awareness', which enhances the quality and experience of our lives.

We've explored Part One of Lama Marut's Two-Part Morning Loll—Gratitude. Part Two serves to remind us of the importance of making the most of each precious day.

Morning Loll Part Two:

None of us knows when our life will end, and getting older, losing resources or becoming sick are all reminders of life's precariousness. But rather than fearing these changes, it's by contemplating impermanence that we become more aware of what matters most. And guess what that leads to? Yes, gratefulness for our lives and the people who make our lives possible.

Like all of us, I've had family and friends who have died. Despite understanding that death is part of the cycle of life—and having studied Buddhism, where contemplating impermanence and 'death awareness' is a key practice—I'm still often taken by surprise when death occurs.

In the past, like many in our culture, I was reluctant to consider death. I was fearful; it all felt so morbid and challenging, and I just didn't want to linger on it. However, with a wiser understanding, we can let go of our fears and appreciate our lives more fully. Death can teach us not to waste the moments that add up to our lives.

I now see that burying my head in the sand is unhelpful, whereas awareness and being realistic add to my gratefulness. It also allows me to appreciate others more, not take them for granted, and reminds me to tell them how much I love and value them.

To 'live every day as if it were your last' is a powerful practice. If we truly thought that today might be our last, we wouldn't waste time being angry, upset, or worried. Instead, we would focus on making the most of it—connecting with those we love and expressing our love, care and appreciation for them. This is something worth remembering as often as possible because none of us knows when that last day will be.

Death awareness does not mean death does not affect us or that we don't care. Rather, it helps us realise the truth of death—that it cannot be fixed or controlled. That realisation opens us up to a deeper level of compassion and wisdom. We don't need to know or fully understand death with our intellect. Instead, we can gently cultivate a relationship with the mystery.

There are three steps in the traditional Buddhist 'death awareness' contemplation:

- Death is certain
- The time of death is uncertain
- What will matter when I die?

These three understandings of death are really contemplations about life. This kind of death awareness has motivated me to make the most of my precious life. In fact, I recall having a student, John, who came to consider this his favourite and most valuable practice too.

Whether it's lolling in bed in the morning, or during a reflective moment in the day, contemplating impermanence and embracing the certainty of death, its uncertain timing, and the importance of living a meaningful life, helps us and others make the most of our time on earth.

Here are some things I reflect on during Part Two of The Morning Loll.

Death is Certain:

> Death happens to all of us. We realise this reality when we recall the people we've known who are no longer with us. Being realistic about our own and others' deaths helps us make the most of life, rather than taking it for granted. Burying our heads in the sand prevents us from having this opportunity.

The Time of Death is Uncertain:

> I want to believe that if I live a healthy life, I'll somehow guarantee a long one. I love to keep fit and do my best to look after my physical wellbeing, hoping that if I'm fortunate enough to reach old age, I won't be a burden.
>
> While it's wise to do our best to live healthily, there are no guarantees that this will extend our lifespan or allow us to reach the average life expectancy. We've all seen examples of healthy people who have suddenly lost

> their health. As we know, there are many ways our life can end, including sickness, accidents or unforeseen circumstances.

A recent holiday in the tropics reminded my partner and me of this. Everywhere we went, warning signs screamed danger: 'Be aware of falling coconuts and tree limbs, crocodiles, cassowaries, marine stingers and snakes!'

While we shouldn't live in constant *fear* of all the possible ways we could die, it's helpful to acknowledge that, even when we take precautions—like following the warning signs and not tempting fate by wading in crocodile habitat—the timing and nature of such events are ultimately beyond our control.

What Will Matter When I Die?

> Many suggest that what will matter to us at the end of life is *how* we have lived. So, if today were our last day, would we look back feeling we'd lived a good life? If not, is there something we could do today to improve that?

Bonnie Ware's *The Top Five Regrets of the Dying: A Life Transformed by the Dearly Departed* [7] offers some insights into how awareness of death can inspire us to live a more compassionate and meaningful life.

For me, living a good life is about kindness. When we do our best to be kind, ethical, and a positive force in the world, we are living a good life!

Awareness of death helps us appreciate life. It's as though an understanding of 'rest in peace', can help us live in peace too.

We can also find and share peace at the end of life too, and that's what we discuss next.

End of Life Advice

During the final stages of a loved one's life, we can provide comfort and meaningful farewells, while letting go of expectations of how things should unfold. Whether expressed outwardly or held quietly within, reflecting on love, forgiveness and gratitude at the end of life can be helpful – both for them and for us.

I had the privilege of being with my parents and my father-in-law during the final stages of their lives, and I'm grateful for the opportunity to have shared that time with them. After receiving helpful advice on being present with those who are dying, I was thankful to draw on that wisdom when the time came to sit with my own parents. I hoped that our time together would be about sharing stories and feelings, and fostering acceptance, forgiveness, and gratitude. However, things don't always go quite the way we want or expect. With my mother, I was reminded to let go of those expectations and simply offer the steady presence she needed.

My mother was a very pragmatic person who had endured many hardships in life and, sadly, had few tools to deal with them. She was, in her own words, 'black and white'—not one for fuss, flowers, or fanfare—and made it quite clear that she did not want to discuss her imminent death or receive any expressions of gratitude. She was also reluctant to talk about memories (even the good ones!) or discuss forgiveness; eye-rolling me with a 'don't give me that rubbish' look whenever what I was saying was not what she needed. So instead, I did my best to remain in peaceful, silent company, making her as physically comfortable as I could. Mum gave me strict guidelines regarding the family getting together for a farewell service— no funeral allowed. Initially, she didn't want me to say anything about her, just the Lord's Prayer. Thankfully, she later reconsidered, allowing me to speak about one thing—family, and how her life was meaningful because of what she considered her greatest achievement: her three children, who were good people, and she was pleased with that.

My dad, on the other hand, was less restrictive, and I was thankful to have many opportunities to share stories, love, forgiveness, and gratitude with him.

Being present with those who are dying

Advice from Lama Marut I took to heart and into the hospital:

- Reassure them of your love and appreciation.
- Let them know you will miss them but that you will be okay—this helps them let go, reassured that you will not fall apart once they've gone.
- Assist them in forgiving those who have harmed them—including forgiving themselves.

I could not talk about these things with my mum, as she didn't want to hear about or discuss such topics: pragmatic, no 'bullshit' and 'black and white' till the end! So, I went through these three advices as internal reflections. I 'thought' them to her, including doing a Tong Len meditation practice which you'll find on the next page. In this practice we use our breath and mind—

breathing in to remove suffering and its causes, and breathing out to send true happiness, love, and its causes.

Once my mother had passed, in my mind and with a quiet whisper, I was able to reassure her that she had done her best, that we loved her, and were all very thankful for all she had given us. I assured her (and myself) that although we would miss her, because of what she had given us, we would be okay. I did not carry on too much, as I knew she would not have liked that.

As the time of death for all is uncertain, some deaths are sudden and we don't always get to be with loved ones during this time. However, whether in person or in our own hearts, at any time we can express our love and appreciation for others, reassure them they don't need to worry about us, forgive them and ourselves, and be kind and grateful. We can do this often and lots. You might like to do it now, or go on to the Tong Len meditation next.

Tong Len Meditation

'Tong Len' is a traditional Buddhist meditation centred around compassion, fostering empathy and a desire to alleviate suffering. This practice promotes well-being and happiness and is widely embraced across spiritual and therapeutic realms.

Tong Len is an ancient form of Buddhist meditation focused on compassion. Engaging in Tong Len meditation helps us connect with, develop and apply compassion in our daily lives. Widely practiced across various spiritual and therapeutic contexts, it cultivates empathy and a willingness to assist others—the cornerstone of our well-being and happiness.

The words 'Tong' and 'Len' are Tibetan terms. 'Long' translates as 'sending out', 'letting go', or 'giving', while 'Len' translates as 'receiving' or 'accepting'. So, what are we receiving, and what are we giving? As radical as it may sound, in this practice we 'receive', or take into our concern, suffering. We then destroy it, and distribute, or 'give out', happiness. Essentially, we accept the unpleasant, obliterate it, and share the good.

This compassion meditation focuses on the desire to alleviate suffering and its causes, and to offer true happiness and its causes. To effectively relieve our own and others' suffering, we must acknowledge its existence. The practice entails a willingness to receive others' suffering with the in-breath, dissolve it using the power of love at the heart, and offer whatever is needed for true happiness and its causes with the out-breath. This is all done meditatively, in the mind.

I find this meditation invaluable when I experience sadness or distress over events such as wars, pandemics, disasters, sickness, or accidents. In such situations, where I often feel helpless, Tong Len reminds me that I can still use the power of the mind to develop compassion and help ease suffering.

The simple on-the-go version is presented below. A more elaborate full meditation version of the Tong Len meditation practice is presented in the Appendix on page 287 and a guided audio is available on mareeallanfowler.com

The on-the-go version of Tong Len:

I can engage in this simple, short on-the-go breath version anytime and anywhere that I perceive suffering—like when I pass someone on the street who looks sad or when I am watching news coverage of people in war-torn areas.

The on-the-go version simply involves:

- A willingness to use the in-breath to remove the suffering perceived. You may be passing someone in the street who looks sad. Simply taking an inbreath and thinking something like 'I remove your sadness/ suffering' as you inhale.'

- In the gap between the in-breath and the out-breath we imagine destroying the suffering, or dissolving it with love—I like to think 'I destroy your suffering with love'. Be sure to have the conviction that the suffering is completely destroyed, not a trace remaining.

- On the out-breath, you send love, true happiness, and its causes. You may like to think something like 'I send you peace and happiness' as you breathe out.

Whichever way I practice Tong Len, this mental contemplation has helped me develop a deeper compassion for myself and for others who are suffering. There are of course other methods, more practical in nature, that we can do to help with any distress or suffering we perceive. We can assist in all sorts of ways including, volunteering or giving our time, money, love and support.

HEART-FRIENDLY WAYS TO PRACTICE

Thank you for reading these reflections and reaching the end of this section on gratitude!

Let's close by expressing this gratitude in some way, perhaps you might like to:

- Write down, draw or speak aloud something you are grateful for.
- Start a gratitude journal.
- Do a 'Thanks, past me' contemplation.
- Do a 'Two-Part Morning Loll'.
- Write a thank-you note to someone.
- Spotlight someone else or yourself!

Ask yourself these fun questions:

'What is one thing I use every day that I rarely stop to be grateful for?' For example, I've chosen my toothbrush: *Thank you, toothbrush and all those involved in its production!*

'When I look around me right now, what is the first thing I see to be grateful for?' I've just noticed my fingers typing this up. *Thank you, finger!*

Who is one person in my life who I might be taking for granted? My partner. *Thank you, E.*

Let's feel glad for all the positive energy we have created together and dedicate this to the happiness and wellbeing of all.

Once we cultivate a grateful heart, we naturally find ourselves wanting to share that abundance, which leads us to the next section on the art of giving.

SOURCES: **WELCOME**

1. Sarah Napthali, *Buddhism For Mothers: A Calm Approach to Caring For Yourself and Your Children*, (Allen and Unwin, 2003)

SOURCES: **SECTION 1. GRATITUDE**

It is thankful people who are happy

2. Francis Bacon, *Positlive quotes*, the Positive.com site: https://positlive.com/its-not-happy-people-who-are-thankful-its-thankful-people-who-are-happy/

Appreciate everything

3. Pema Chödrön, *When Things Fall Apart: Heart Advices For Difficult Times*, (Boston Shambhala, 2002).

'Mother' – Expanding our understanding

4. *The Oxford English Dictionary*, Mother definition: https://www.oed.com/dictionary/mother_n1?tl=true#:~:text=1.-,a.,a%20stepmother, Entry 1.4a

5. Mother Teresa https://www.goodreads.com/author/quotes/838305.Mother_Teresa

6. Meggan Waterson, *Mary Magdalene Revealed*, (Hay House, 2019).

The Top Five Regrets of the Dying

7. Bonnie Ware, *The Top Five Regrets of the Dying: A Life Transformed by the Dearly Departed*, (Hay House, 2019)

2. GIVING & RECEIVING

GIVING & RECEIVING

Giving generously from a place of love, wisdom and without expectation feels great, beautifully connecting both giver and receiver. Here we'll explore the art of giving and receiving through fun ideas, including 'Smonsering' and 'Secret Santa'. We'll also explore how to be more open to receiving, including asking for help when needed.

Catching the Generosity Bug

Amid life's challenges, being generous transforms the ordinary. From unexpected donations to heartfelt connections, the joy of giving and receiving is worth spreading.

It's funny how, when we're on the lookout for something, we suddenly see it everywhere—like noticing a particular model or colour of a car once we've decided to buy a similar one. The same applies to how we see people. When we focus on what's wrong, that's what fills our vision. But, when we deliberately look for kindness, generosity begins to appear everywhere—and not just around us, but within us too.

One wintry morning during the bleak days of COVID, I was working at the Mission offering breakfast to those in need. The normally warm dining room was temporarily closed and we were only allowed to serve takeaway breakfasts from the shop door. It was bitterly cold and everyone was feeling the stress of the COVID lockdown. I noticed my mood slipping with each gust of wind, so I made a conscious effort to focus on the positive.

It didn't take long for generosity to show up.

The first was from a construction worker who came to the serving door and handed over a generous cash donation, He said, 'I've been working in the street all week watching you guys help these people and I wanted to help too.' We all warmed right up after that, so uplifted to receive his kindness and I could see that he felt the same in offering it. It was a heartwarming exchange of dignity, gratitude and goodwill.

The second act of generosity was also a donation of money for the Mission. This time it was from a woman who had just dropped her 22-year-old daughter at the hospital for her first chemo treatment. How she was able to think of others when her own daughter was also so in need touched and inspired us. She shared stories about her daughter and we could see our brief connection gave her a lift as well.

Now that I was looking for it, generosity popped up in so many other ways that day too. A steady line of people thanked us with encouraging compliments, told us to 'take care', gave us smiles, and asked how we were doing. It showed me that giving doesn't need to be a grand gesture, or cost anything at all. We can all give in some way—through our attention, a listening ear, our skills or expertise, or simply our friendliness.

In all its forms, giving has the capacity to uplift both the giver and the receiver. In the chapters ahead, we'll explore the many ways we can create a healthy epidemic of it in our everyday lives.

Give Without Expectation

True generosity involves giving freely without expecting anything in return. Despite this, it can be challenging not to seek gratitude. My personal story explores this balance and the eventual inner peace that arose when I let go.

Nelson Mandela tells us that, 'There can be no greater gift than that of giving our time and energy to help others without expecting anything in return'. [1]

Although this reflects the true spirit of generosity, it can be a tricky experience for us non-Mandelas in our day-to-day lives. That's because it feels so good to receive at least a thank you in response to an act of kindness. But sometimes there is absolutely no acknowledgement of the time, thought or energy we have given. We often see this play out on our roads when a driver slows down to kindly let another driver in, but when no friendly, thankful gesture is received, then gets upset.

I had a similar experience recently when I sent POM's handmade 'loved and appreciated' care packages to staff and students I used to work with at a school boarding house. I love spreading the 'loved and appreciated' message and thought it would be meaningful to share it with this community going through a very different and difficult senior school experience due to the COVID restrictions.

I prepared a small gift for each of the thirty-two staff and students: some POM biscuits and a 'loved and appreciated' face washer*. I left the box on the doorstep of the boarding house.

Looking back, this gift selection was obviously not high on the priority list for senior school girls. I checked in with my intention for doing this, making sure it wasn't about me needing thanks, or to be seen as good person, or liked. No, it wasn't. I simply wanted to spread the positive 'loved and appreciated' message with them.

So, I let go of any expectation of appreciation and instead rested in my kind intention. Or so I thought. The longer the lack of acknowledgement went on, the louder my inner voice of self-doubt and criticism rose: 'Was it a stupid thing to do?'. 'Do they not like me?' 'What was I thinking?' Embarrassment and insecurity swelled.

I needed to return to my wise self for the reminder that at its core, it was a kind thing to do, with a kind intention. So, I thanked and acknowledged myself, completely letting go the need for outside thanks or appreciation. That change enabled the return of my peace of mind. A few days later I received an unexpected message of thanks from a staff member. This was the now unnecessary icing on top of the thank-you cake I'd already gifted myself.

** The knitting pattern for the cotton washcloth is available at mareeallanfowler.com*

Wise Giving

Though generosity is a beautiful thing to do, if we consistently offer something and get no response, it's possible our giving is placing a burden on the recipient. Perhaps we're providing something unwanted or unnecessary.

Our giving may also sometimes enable negative behaviour, fostering dependency or reinforcing a lack of responsibility in another. In this case it may be necessary to find other ways to help or support that are less harmful, such as supporting their agency rather than rescuing them, offering support though not necessarily solutions, or redirecting them to other options.

We can also be mindful of when we're tempted to give beyond our means and capabilities either emotionally, financially or energetically. It doesn't matter if we're motivated by a desire to be liked or to be seen as a good person, doing so may hurt ourselves, our families or others. Regularly checking in with ourselves, reflecting on our intentions and doing a stocktake of our resources helps ensure our generosity remains caring, sustainable and wise.

One of the most sustainable things we can offer to people is a smile and a compliment, and that's what the next chapter is all about.

Resting Smiley Face

Dive into the delightful world of spreading smiles and compliments. Discover the magic where a simple smile can transform worlds, creating ripples of positivity.

I'm continually awed by the quiet power of smiles, and how something so small and free can brighten someone's day at any moment.

Smiles transcend language barriers and cultural differences, offering an immediate way to connect. They create moments of happiness at home, foster goodwill in business, and gently bridge the space between friends and strangers alike. The simple act of smiling lifts not only our own mood, but also that of those who receive it. Add a heartfelt compliment, and the delight multiplies. I've come to enjoy sharing a crinkly-eyed smile with anyone I pass, without expecting it to be returned—although it usually is. This practice felt especially meaningful during the masked COVID years, when people could still sense a smile, even beneath a mask.

Around that time someone told me I have a *'resting smiling face'*—a comment that lit up my smile even more, affirming as it did that my improving inner contentment reflected outwardly.

As an anonymous quote wisely observes, 'Making one person smile can change the world—maybe not the whole world, but their world.' And in doing so, it often changes ours too.
When we reflect on the dynamics of karma—the continual unfolding of cause and effect—we're reminded that small, positive actions matter. A shared smile plants a seed of goodwill,

one that may bloom long after the moment has passed. In this way, a smile can profoundly improve someone else's day—and our own.

Even thinking about smiling can bring one to our face. And I'm grinning right now thinking about my favourite quotes about smiles:

> Douglas Horton once said, **'Smile—it's free therapy.'**
> Mother Teresa reminds us that **'Peace begins with a smile.'**
> And Dolly Parton offers the generous advice: **'If you see someone without a smile, give 'em yours.'**

And it's worth smiling, because smiling:

- lifts mood and fosters positivity
- relieves stress
- supports immune health
- enhances approachability
- requires less effort than frowning
- costs nothing, yet creates much
- enriches the receiver without impoverishing the giver.

Compliments are equally wonderful to bestow, as well as to receive. My lovely next-door neighbour, Maree, frequently compliments my attire, noticing the effort I put into my appearance. My experience of her generosity in offering these compliments reinforces how good it feels to uplift others. Undoubtedly, she experiences a sense of fulfilment too by spreading positivity, just as we do when we make others feel good.

While compliments on appearance are one example, we can also compliment actions, words, or strengths. I'm using the word 'compliment' rather than 'praise' here as I like to avoid using praising phrases such as 'you are such a good girl, for doing that.' We are often unaware that using praise in this way can be experienced as manipulative or condescending. Maybe I'm being pedantic, but for me it feels very different when someone says, 'I really like what you've done; that helps me a lot'; followed by thanks rather than 'you're a good girl for doing that'.

American author Joyce Meyer's advice to 'Compliment people. Magnify others' strengths and not their weaknesses' [2] resonates with me too. Hearing that I've done a commendable job brings me immense joy. It's also important to compliment ourselves, emphasising our strengths over our perceived weaknesses.

Striving to be a kind and encouraging friend—to others and to ourselves irrespective of the circumstances—helps sustain our collective well-being.

How to build on this well-being by being a 'daymaker' is covered in the next chapter.

Be a Daymaker

In David Wagner's delightful read, *Life as a Daymaker*, [3] he unveils the art of intentional goodwill. Being a daymaker through simple acts creates positive upward spirals in the world.

David Wagner defines a 'daymaker' as 'a person who performs acts of kindness with the intention of making the world a better place.' The key principle is that making someone's day with a kind act, makes our own day, too. While David prefers to call these gestures 'intentional acts of goodwill' rather than 'random acts of kindness', I try to practice both.

There is great power in being 'the change we want to see in the world'. When we act with kindness, we begin to perceive ourselves and others as kinder, and the world itself as a kinder place—setting in motion the very causes that allow it to be so.

I love it when someone responds to something kind I've done or a compliment I've given with: 'You've made my day!' This happened recently when I complimented a mother on the great job she was doing juggling the safety of four kids on bikes and scooters, and again when I went back to thank a barista for making a great coffee. This is what David Wagner refers to as being a 'daymaker.'

I often forget how incredibly easy it is to give someone a lift by being a daymaker myself. Often, all it takes is a smile, a compliment, a small act of kindness, or a word of encouragement. We can also be our own daymakers. For example, when in need of a boost, we can check in with our wise self for some kind, encouraging words and brighten our own day!

Sometimes I catch myself thinking that I need to do something big or heroic to really make a difference, but I'm regularly reminded that small acts of kindness can be just as powerful. And as we never really know what someone else is dealing with on any given day, a simple compliment, a kind word, or a small supportive gesture can massively shift the tone of their day.

That certainly happened one rainy afternoon when I said to a passer-by, 'Your orange raincoat looks great—it's cheered me up.' I had no idea that such a small comment would brighten her day—and lift me up as well.

When we understand that the secret to our own happiness and a meaningful life is linked to making others happy, it becomes easier to do these small things; to be daymakers. Whether we can actually give someone a boost is not in our control, but seeing ourselves make efforts is where the happy perception of ourselves begins. So, let's create a positive upward spiral for all.

Giving With Love

Embracing Mother Teresa's wisdom that giving is about love, not quantity, we can discover joy in meaningful, stress-free generosity beyond occasions.

Every year as Christmas creeps closer, I notice a familiar unease about how commercial it all feels. At times I even feel stingy and want to withdraw from participating. But when I recall Mother Teresa's wisdom: 'It's not how much we give, but how much love we put into giving.' [4] I'm able to reconnect with the true spirit of Christmas.

When we infuse love into our giving as Mother Teresa suggests—no matter whether it's for Christmas, birthdays, anniversaries or other special occasions—we contemplate the person who will receive the gift. By doing this, we can find deep satisfaction in selecting, creating, or doing something special for them.

When I tune into my wise self and follow this approach, I'm able to accept my discomfort with the commercialisation of Christmas but am also able to embrace the joy of it without the stress of a shopping frenzy. It's all about how I frame my thoughts and how I act, so I focus on the opportunity to be generous, giving in a variety of ways through handmade items, shared time, simple acts of kindness and yes, some carefully chosen commercial gifts.

And, when we're the ones receiving, we get to feel the thoughtfulness and generosity of time, money and care that have gone into what's being given to us. Of course, giving isn't limited to occasions like Christmas and birthdays; it's enjoyable to be a giver anytime.

'Smonsering' and the Joy of Giving Secretly

Embrace the joy of giving through Smonsering and Kris Kringle. Whether it's handmade gifts or secret acts of kindness, giving with love transforms the experience.

When I first heard the word 'Smonsering' I had no idea what it meant, and I still don't know its origins, but what I do know is that it's a very fun way to give!

I was introduced to the concept when working with a team of twelve in an Occupational Therapy department. They explained that Smonsering is all about doing kind things for each other in secret.

The idea was simple: each person drew a name out of a hat, and the person they picked became their Smonser. For the next week, the goal was to do something kind for that person each day, but secretly. Desks were decorated, cups of tea appeared, edible treats and thoughtful gifts specific to the person were all given anonymously. Good surprises mysteriously appeared on desks all day. It was such a gratifying thing to do, and equally enjoyable to observe others sneaking around to perform so many kind, creative and generous acts.

Secret Santa (or Kris Kringle) is another fun way to give and allows us to give and receive presents in work or family group situations. There is often a price limit or other guidelines, and in our family, we have an interesting variation: the Home-Made Kris Kringle where the gifts need to be made by the giver.

I really enjoy my family's creations each year and the delight on their faces as they describe the gifts and how they made them.

At times, I can feel a little stressed or intimidated by my creative family though, and struggle to think of something to make in return. However, when I accept the feeling of performance anxiety and tune into my wise self, I'm reminded that:

- When we put love into our giving, we can think about the person and tune in to what would be just right for them and make them happy.
- It's fun to have a go at being creative with gift making.
- I can let go of high or unrealistic expectations and just do my best within my capabilities to make something my recipient would love.
- If my gift is infused with love and I've done my best to make it, I can give it and let go of how it is received.

All sorts of wonderful gifts have been made by my family over the years, including knitted slippers (which went on to inspire the POM Mouse slippers), a gingham playsuit which matches the curtains on our camper, personalised postcards and playing cards, chopping boards, vinyl records, family recipe books, pottery pieces, and more.

I'm reminded that giving need not be restricted to Christmas, family or workplaces either. Norman Wesley Brooks, author of the Christmas poem *Let Every Day Be Christmas*, states that 'Christmas is forever, not just one day. For loving, sharing, giving are not put away.' [5]

It can be so fun to give, but learning how to receive is also a gift! Let's discuss that in the next chapter.

Connecting Through Giving and Receiving

Giving creates meaningful connection, and it's important for us to embrace both roles of giver and receiver in this dynamic exchange.

We connect with other through being both a giver and a receiver. This connection fosters a sense of belonging.

In my Buddhist studies I learned an invaluable lesson: a giver and a receiver exist interdependently—just like we do in life. There can be no giver without someone to give to, and there can be no receiver without someone to receive from. They make each other possible. The energetic connection between them is the act of giving, which creates a new sense of belonging.

One way we can miss this opportunity for connection is by being unwilling to play the role of either receiver or giver. Obviously, when we feel stingy and don't want to give, we can experience a sense of disconnection. But just as often, if we deny a gift, an opportunity is lost too. We know how it feels to do something kind for someone, only to hear responses like, 'You shouldn't have done that', 'That's embarrassing', or 'It was too generous, unnecessary'.

I have expressed this very sentiment myself, effectively shutting down someone's generosity because I felt embarrassed or unworthy. One day, when I was feeling low, a friend kindly bought me flowers. I said, 'You shouldn't have done that, I don't deserve them,' and gave them back to her! This response left me feeling worse, and my friend confused. I had missed an opportunity for connection.

This type of response can stem from feelings of worthlessness, or from a learned habit of rejecting kindness. It might even be pride, resisting the vulnerability of accepting someone's effort to lift us up. Whatever the reason, blocking this exchange of kindness hinders the joy of connecting, receiving, and being generous. It may also reinforce unhelpful and untrue feelings we hold about ourselves.

With awareness, we can change this unhelpful habit, bringing greater joy and gratitude to both parties.

When I feel embarrassed or unworthy of receiving a gift and am tempted to say something like, 'You shouldn't have done that', I try instead to pause, accept the feeling, and tune into my wise self to be reminded that we are all equal, worthy, and unique—and to accept the gift with gratitude. In this way, the giver also becomes a receiver of my gratitude, and I become a giver of thanks, deepening our connection. It's a win-win.

But what if it's help, rather than a gift, we need to give or accept? Join me in the next chapter to explore this concept.

Accepting Help

Helping and being helped are two sides of the same coin. Consistently refusing assistance, or overstepping in offering it, denies opportunities for connection and growth.

I've realised that I sometimes shut down another's generosity by refusing their help. This tendency comes from an untrue and unhelpful belief that it's important to always be 'independent'.

The truth is we are all *interdependent* and cannot survive a second without the kindness of others in all areas of our lives. Of course, it's important we take responsibility for doing things ourselves, but consistently refusing help can be unwise and potentially unkind. It not only denies others the opportunity to feel good about giving but also denies us the chance to be supported and to feel grateful for it.

Recently I watched an older woman attempting to board a tram with a small wheelie case. She had carried it from the curb and appeared capable of lifting it onto the tram herself, yet a man approached and asked if he could help. She graciously accepted, and I could see they were both happy with the exchange.

It was inspiring to observe how the woman's gracious acceptance of help created a moment of connection. It was also noteworthy to see the man's respectful approach in asking if help was needed.

Sometimes I do the opposite: barging in to help without checking to see if my help is wanted. If we're attached to the identity of being a giving or helpful person, we may miss signals that our offering is a burden or intrusion. In such cases, it's worth pausing to check our motivation: are we simply trying to look good? Are we overreaching, trying to fix someone or something that isn't ours to fix? Are we inserting ourselves into a situation or imposing solutions to something beyond our control? These attempts to help—however well-intentioned—can sometimes be quite unhelpful!

At such times, it may be more appropriate to practice anonymous giving or offer a silent Tong Len blessing (on page 38) in our mind and heart. In other situations, it's enough to simply ask if help is needed: if it is, then do your best to assist, and if it's not, accept a decline graciously. At other times still, the wisest move is to wait—to perhaps stand aside and allow others to help.

Check in with your wise self and you will know what to do.

Sometimes you may be the one in the position of needing help, and we discuss how to ask for help next.

Asking for Help

When it comes to asking for help, I do my best to be strong enough to be independent, wise enough to know when I need support, and courageous enough to ask for it. Here's why it matters.

I can sometimes be stubborn when it comes to asking for help. Again, that untrue belief that 'I always need to be independent and do it all myself' is at play. This unhelpful mindset robs me of the support I need, denies others the opportunity and joy of helping, and can cause me stress and frustration.

When I was organising retreats and workshops for my teachers, I sometimes slipped into this unhelpful 'I need to do it all myself' attitude. This would result in me running around like crazy—stressed, resentful, and tired—with the burning smell of martyr lingering in the air. Others in our retreat group were willing and perfectly capable of helping. Over time, I learned to ask for help and delegate, which made the process far more fun for everyone.

When asking for help, I try to do so without the expectation of others being available, of it being completed within certain time frames, or to an unrealistic standard.

If help is available, I try to give clear explanations, let go of perfectionism, and express gratitude. I recall Lama Marut saying, 'Expectation is disappointment in training', which reminds me it's much better for our mind to *anticipate* a good outcome, rather than *expect* it.

It can be tricky when we ask for help and others are unable to assist. In these moments, I try to be understanding, letting go of both expectation and judgment as we don't know what others are dealing with or their timelines. Instead, we can seek help elsewhere or accept the situation and choose to complete the task ourselves with joy, rather than resentment. Ultimately, if we can't do something on our own, we may need to let go of the project entirely. Remember, we have the choice.

There's a sweet spot when we ask for help and others respond positively, or when someone asks for our help and we are able to offer it. When generosity flows freely and love, kindness and connection grow between us, it's a moment to rejoice in.

HEART-FRIENDLY WAYS TO PRACTICE

Thank you for reading these reflections and reaching the end of this section on giving!

Let's give ourselves the gift of contemplation and take a moment to reflect through the thoughts that follow.

- How can we be more generous toward others—creatively, anonymously or simply with a smile?
- How might we be brave enough to ask others for help when we need it?
- How might we show ourselves greater generosity by seeking support?
- Think of someone who could do with an uplift and plan some way to compliment, encourage or give them a small gift.

Finally, let's give ourselves a smile and a compliment for taking some time for reflection.

Let's feel glad for all the positive energy we have created together and dedicate this to the happiness and wellbeing of all.

Giving Time and energy without expectation of return

1. Nelson Mandala, *Quote Fancy*, https://quotefancy.com/quote/874304/Nelson-Mandela-There-can-be-no-greater-gift-than-that-of-giving-one-s-time-and-energy-to

2. Joyce Meyer, *Quote Fancy*: https://quotefancy.com/quote/846018/Joyce-Meyer-Compliment-people-Magnify-their-strengths-not-their-weaknesses

Be a daymaker

3. David Wagner, *Life As a Daymaker; How to Change the World by Making Someone's Day*, (Jadene Group, 2003).

Put love into giving

4. Mother Teresa, *Quote Fancy*, https://quotefancy.com/quote/874304/Nelson-Mandela-There-can-be-no-greater-gift-than-that-of-giving-one-s-time-and-energy-to

Let every day be like Christmas

5. Norman Wesley Brooks, *Let Every Day Be Christmas*, https://www.quotegarden.com/let-every-day-be-christmas-norm-brooks.html

3. FOUNDATIONAL PRACTICES

**A Toolkit to a Happier Life:
ABCD, On Each Shoulder, and the Four Forces**

FOUNDATIONAL PRACTICES

In this section I share a few practices I've come to see as truly foundational for shifting unhelpful ways of thinking and being. I encourage you to spend some time with them and let them settle in as we'll keep coming back to these ideas throughout the book given they're central to cultivating peace, clarity, and contentment.

We'll start with **awareness**—a simple but powerful skill that helps us notice what's going on, accept our feelings as they arise, and gently question the thoughts we believe with little scrutiny. From there, I'll introduce **ABCD**, an easy way to tap into our inner wisdom and choose a wiser response; **On Each Shoulder**, a playful way to work with both the unhelpful ego voice and the wiser self; and the **Four Forces**, a conscience-clearing practice that supports inner ease.

Think of these as tools you can return to again and again—in everyday moments, and especially when things feel a bit challenging.

The ABCD Practice

People of all ages can benefit from learning the ABCD Practice as it helps us find and respond with emotional balance.

I think of the ABCD practice as a kind of emotional first aid kit and it's something I reach for when a feeling or situation flares up. It prompts us to check in with our wise selves for guidance, helping us deal more healthily with our feelings, emotions and thoughts.

The first step is simply noticing that we've been triggered. This is about being *aware that* something someone has said or done (the 'someone' can also include ourselves!) has left us with feelings of anger, irritation, jealousy, hurt, or sadness.

This awareness helps us pause before we ignore, bypass, squash the feeling down or fuel it with negative stories. *Awareness* limits the opportunity for justification or blame, making it much less likely we'll react inappropriately with a knee-jerk response.

Once we're *aware* of the triggered feeling, emotion or associated thoughts, we can do our ABCD.

A is for Accepting the feeling, thought or situation.

Honour your experience by holding it lightly, befriending it and allowing yourself to feel it. Try not to suppress what's there, react impulsively, or feed it with blame, criticism, justification, or harsh self-talk. It's simply about letting it be.

B is for Breathing.

> Take a few slow, steady breaths. As you breathe, continue to gently feel and befriend what's arising. Allow the thoughts and feelings to move through you and release them. That creates space for the next step.

C is for Connecting.

> Now, connect with your wise, intuitive self—often felt around the heart. You might silently ask, 'What's the wisest way to respond here?' or 'What's needed right now?'

D is for Doing—and giving thanks.

> Act on the guidance that arises, and take a moment to offer thanks—for the insight, the pause, or the opportunity to respond more wisely.

When we follow these steps, the intensity of the feeling can soften and we will know how to respond. Sometimes when I do the ABCD I'm guided to what I need to do, think, say, or let go of. Sometimes it means doing nothing at all, and sometimes I continue with the breathwork a little longer.

In everyday moments, when we're busy or on the go, we can use ABCD in a very simple, shorthand way. We start by noticing we're triggered, then briefly accept what's present, take a breath or two, connect with our wiser self, and respond.

With practice, this process often becomes even more natural. Sometimes a single mindful breath is enough to reconnect with our inner wisdom and sense what to do next.

We'll experiment with these versions in the reflections ahead.

A Meditation for Checking In to My Wise Self

This meditation is a longhand version of ABCD. It's a way of grounding oneself before connecting with the wise self within. I often do it in our POM yoga classes and in times of uncertainty.

I practice this meditation regularly, especially when I'm at a crossroads and feeling unsure about what to do in life. I begin with some meditation preliminaries to help ground me in the here and now and to quiet my mind. The preliminaries, described in more detail on page 165 and also available on mareeallanfowler.com, can include checking my posture so I'm comfortable and then I take three long, deep inhales through the nostrils and exhales through the mouth before moving into the Checking In to My Wise Self Meditation.

1. **Bring awareness to what you're feeling**
   Gently bring to mind a part of yourself that is experiencing a particular emotion or associated worry or stress. Maybe you've felt anxious, sad, lonely, or confused over something that has been going on. Like all of us, I've had times when I've felt angry over an injustice, sad about a loss, or confused about the best decision to make, and I am unsure of what to do. This meditation is about acknowledging and accepting that part of ourselves and checking in with our wise selves for guidance.

2. **Take an intentional breath down to the heart.**
   Imagine yourself connecting with the energy of love,

or your wise self at the heart centre—and continue to breathe. Feel into the love and connection there. Settle into that centred, peaceful and loved feeling.

3. **Deepen the connection**
   Take another intentional breath and continue to deepen your connection to the heart. As you keep breathing, gently ask your wise self for guidance.

Often, I find simply breathing into the heart and connecting with love and wisdom is enough. Sometimes, a kind, encouraging word or sentence comes up. Other times, I feel little, but I trust that wisdom is there, accessible and available when needed. Sometimes clarity arises afterwards, hours or days after the meditation.

4. **Close with gratitude.**
   Take one final, deep, intentional breath—a big breath of gratitude. Continue to fill the body and mind with gratitude as you reflect on what you are thankful for.

When I'm closing with gratitude, I often think of:

- Teachers: without their kindness and generosity, we could not access wisdom.
- My internal wise self and human self: My human self is my wise self's chance to be here. Truly human, truly divine, both of them. We are a team.
- All those people in my life, including loved ones (and those I don't even know) who make my amazing life possible: People who provide daily necessities and much, much more.

I find that closing with gratitude opens my perspective, releasing some of the tension around the original worry.

'On Each Shoulder': A Meditation for Dealing with Self-Criticism

'On Each Shoulder' is another way I like to think about tuning into the wise self. I imagine two aspects of myself perched on each of my shoulders—the self-critical aspects of our ego, on the right and my wise self on the left. Balancing these aspects with awareness and kindness can transform negative thoughts into supportive insights.

When working with difficult thoughts, I find it useful to imagine that on one shoulder (l like to think the right), sits an unhelpful part of my ego. This can include the critical taskmaster part of me. This overprotective side aims to keep me safe but often chimes in with overblown and fearful intrusive thoughts such as: You might fail if you attempt that/You're not good enough/You always make mistakes/You shouldn't't forgive them/You need to work hard to get others to approve of you. And of course, 'You need to stress about this'.

My critical task master compares me to others (usually unfavourably), is unforgiving, worries about things, and drives me very hard. Instead of trying to suppress, banish or defeat these protective, critical, or taskmaster-like thought habits, I find it much more helpful to accept them kindly and seek to befriend them. It's never helpful to suppress them or to let them take over. I say something to myself like 'thank you for sharing', that way it feels heard and I can check in instead to hear my wise self, offering some kind advice on what to do. *Awareness*, a friendly

Acceptance and some *Breaths* to allow them to pass through, gives the space to Connect with and hear our wise intuitive selves.

In Buddhism, critical and destructive thoughts are known as mental afflictions because they disturb our peace of mind. They can also be referred to as 'intrusive' thoughts. The good news is that rather than attacking these thoughts with return attacks or suppression, we can work with kindness to befriend them, promoting our peace of mind. While many of these fearful thoughts may serve as warnings intended to protect us, instead of believing them, we can recognise that they offer an opportunity to shine the light of wisdom on them.

Critical thought patterns may have developed during childhood to protect ourselves from threats or to get our needs for safety, acceptance, and love met. Or perhaps they stem from repressed anger turned inward. By considering them as invitations to accept, befriend and replace with truth, we can use kindness and self-encouragement to restore our peace of mind.

Now, let's talk about who is on the other shoulder, the left one. It is our wise, intuitive self, which can be called by many names, including our 'best friend self', 'Buddha nature', 'soul, 'God', 'basic goodness', 'wise self', or 'universal wisdom'. Whatever term we choose, it represents the beyond-words wisdom we all possess.

We need to be aware and listen for our wise self because the taskmaster or overprotective side of our ego often drowns it out. In Buddhism, discernment involves knowing what to 'take up' and what to 'give up'. Practices and habits conducive to our peace of mind, such as forgiveness, are good to take up. Practices that harm and disturb our peace of mind, such as refusing to forgive or being critical of ourselves, are those to give up. For me, discernment means listening to my wise, intuitive best friend self on my left shoulder and learning to befriend and work kindly with the punitive, critical taskmaster or overprotective personality on the right. It's a friendly dialogue between these two aspects of myself. In my day-to-day life, for example, when I'm ready to press send on a blog I've written, it sounds something like this:

> Taskmaster: 'In posting that blog you might offend someone, are you really qualified to say that?'
>
> Wise Self: 'Thank you for sharing, I know you're trying to keep me safe, but it's okay, I'm going to send it as others might find it helpful.'

As the upcoming reflections explore, befriending these parts of ourselves with a friendly dialogue of acceptance and love is a work in progress. Just keeping the conversation going!

Clearing Our Conscience with The 'Four Forces' Practice

The Buddhist practice known as the 'Four Opponent Powers of Purification', or 'Four Forces', offers a path to mindfully restore inner harmony, cultivate peace and develop more beneficial behaviours.

Have you ever regretted doing something? I certainly have. Sometimes the thought of our past actions can niggle and nag at us over days and years, destroying our peace of mind. I've found the Four Forces to be an invaluable way to deal with these regrets. This simple practice helps us clear our conscience and make amends for things we wish we hadn't done. It's a powerful practice to restore our sense of peace.

The Buddhist purification practice called the 'Four Opponent Powers of Purification' is traditionally used to purify negative karmas or misdeeds we regret. My teacher, Lama Marut [1], adapted this method to be more accessible and memorable, drawing from *A Complete Guide to the Buddhist Path.* [2] He named his version the Four Forces—framing it as a purification, making amends or conscience-clearing practice. In his approach, each force or step begins with the letter R: Refuge, Regret, Restraint, and Recompense.

Traditionally, this practice is applied in relation to the Ten Buddhist Ethical Guidelines (outined in Section 4: 'Causality/ Karma', on page 104, and Section 5: 'Ten Guidelines for a Good Life' on page 132. The following reflections demonstrate though how we can home bake with the Four Forces to live a good life.

It's such a useful practice I'll refer to this Four Forces practice throughout the book.

To even begin, we must first **acknowledge** and **admit** that we have done something we regret. Then we move through the four steps:

1. Refuge:

Let's think about 'refuge' in terms of finding an inner comfort, safety or grounding that will help us work with what we regret. We take refuge in the understanding that we have done something that's not in alignment with our highest values and that there will be consequence because karma is at play, 'what goes around comes around'. For example, if we have been rude to someone, we understand that karmically we will experience the perception of someone being rude to us in the future. The workings of karma are complex, so we don't know how or when this will occur, but something has made the imprint.

We also take refuge knowing that we have seen ourselves do this particular action, and it will weigh on our conscience, adversely affecting our peace of mind. Put simply, we don't want to be the kind of person who behaves this way again and we want to change the pattern. Taking refuge is about taking responsibility for our actions, taking safety in our understanding of karma or causality, and doing something that helps us learn and grow. Like this practice!

2. Regret:

This step is the genuine feeling of wishing we had not done, said, or even thought a particular thing. It's not about self-hatred or guilt; it's simply acknowledging that this is not the person we want to be. (We will look at the difference between this and 'guilt regret' in the next chapter).

3. Restraint:

Here we commit to restraining and refraining from repeating the action for a reasonable amount of time. Make this realistic and doable. Saying 'I am never going to do this again' may set ourselves up to fail.

4. Recompense:

Involves devising a little activity that makes amends for the action. It's completely up to us what we decide to do. It can just involve you and your mind and doesn't even need to be expressed—although sometimes an apology, acts of generosity or kindness can go a long way. We are our own judge and jury.

Recompense can involve forgiving the other person and forgiving ourselves, too. Once we perform the recompense activity, we can tell ourselves we have purified the misdeed, removing it from our conscience.

Lama Marut adds a bonus fifth force to the Four Forces—Rejoice!

5. Rejoice:

This final step is all about feeling happy we have done this practice to make amends and clear our conscience. It is always good to rejoice in goodness, including our own and this step reminds us to do so and enjoy the moment.

I once heard a story about a Buddhist Vietnamese American soldier who had been fighting with the US army during the Vietnam war. When the soldier returned home, while he knew he had not actively killed anyone, he was concerned he might have accidentally killed someone when firing into the scrub. He knew that killing was the top misdeed and expressed his concern to his Buddhist teacher.

His teacher gave him this Four Forces practice. The soldier certainly had Refuge in his understanding of what it meant to have killed someone and Regretted this possible action. His teacher gave him a Restraint and Recompense practice of restraining from taking life for the rest of his life. The Recompense activity was looking after a sheep in his backyard for the duration of the sheep's life. In taking on the care of the sheep until its natural death, the soldier had cleared his conscience and lived with peace of mind. The rescued sheep had a great life too!

Next, we'll explore how guilt and regret differ.

How to Know If You're Dealing with Guilt or Regret

The Four Forces offers a path to purify misdeeds, clear our conscience and restore inner peace. Understanding the difference between debilitating guilt and beneficial regret offers a transformative journey towards self-improvement.

Do you know the difference between unhelpful guilt and helpful regret? I didn't, and somehow, I thought it was noble to feel guilty and beat myself up with criticism and guilt over unkind things I wished I hadn't done. Lama Marut helped me understand the difference and introduced me to the Four Forces, as outlined in these reflections.

When my intention has been to be kind, such as when I have truly wanted to help someone, I can rest in that kind intention regardless of the result. But, what do I do about the times I have not had a kind intention, such as when I've been angry, wanted to get back at someone for a perceived wrong, or the times I've been self-righteous, judgmental, selfish, unforgiving or critical? For those I can't rest in the knowledge my original intention was kind, so what do I do?

Although I've wallowed in guilt many times, that, and berating ourselves, is not the solution. Why? Because guilt keeps us from learning and growing.

Lama Marut suggested that guilt is just an excuse to give ourselves a hard time while doing nothing about it. Guilt is 'all about me': what a bad person I am, what a terrible thing I've done. Continually rehashing the past and berating ourselves is of no use to anyone because when we're busy with all that negative self-talk, we destroy our peace of mind, confidence, and happiness and are not available to others.

So, how do we stop this unhelpful habit of broken-record thinking? We practice regret instead of guilt and move through the Four (or Five) Forces. This purification practice allows us to do something about our feelings of regret. With regret, we admit we have done something harmful and acknowledge we are not happy about having done it. Regret implies the intention we will do something to make up for what we have done. Enter Recompense.

From Road Rage to Happy Motoring—The Four Forces in Action

In this reflection, I share how I used the Four Forces practice to transform my road rage into happy motoring in a flash.

Do you ever let a small resentment, like a horn 'toot' in traffic, build up and ruin your peace of mind and day? For me, when something irritating happens, I can really stew over it, making myself and others miserable. 'They should not have said or done that (irritating thing)' plays on repeat. The truth, though, is that it happened—it's like this now—and no amount of protest that it should be different will change it.

So, let's think about helpful ways to deal with these little misdeeds, things we regret doing and those things done to us. These strategies can prevent regrets and resentments from replaying in our minds and building into bigger ones that ruin our present and future peace of mind.

The Four Forces is a very helpful conscience-clearing exercise, especially useful for small resentments and regrets.

I remember many years ago applying the Four Forces when I was driving along Punt Road on my way to Northcote to check out a yoga studio for an event I was organising. I sped through a yellow light when I could have stopped in time. This made it very difficult for a motorist turning right, and he let me know with a horn blast.

Immediately I felt sorry about what I'd done and, of course, also tried to justify it in my mind. But I knew I'd done the wrong thing. I was also tempted to get cross at the motorist for his blast—more justification, excuses, and blame. Instead, thankfully, I remembered a couple of things.

Rather than berate myself for being selfish, boarding the worry-thought-train, or beating myself up with guilt, I reminded myself: there is never a good time to worry. That if I could do something about it, I could do the Four Forces. But if there was nothing I could do, to let it go.

Awareness was of huge help here. I tuned into my wise self with an ABCD and asked:

- Are those thoughts true?
- Am I fundamentally a careless, selfish driver?
- Are other motorists *always* having a go at me?
- Is this thought helpful to me and helping me be happier and more available to others?

The answer to all these questions was a resounding NO, so I was able to rewrite my thinking using the Four Forces.

The Four Forces are akin to 'mind gardening' or conscience clearing. As with any garden, if we attend to our mind garden regularly, it won't become overwhelmed and out of control. Instead, it will be more tranquil, growing abundant beautiful thoughts and intentions. Here's how I mind-gardened, applying the Four Forces in the running-the-yellow-light situation.

Refuge

Firstly, I admitted it. Foolish justifications aside, I could have stopped safely at that yellow light. I then considered what brings me comfort, acknowledging that not considering others opposes the positive, happy force I want to be. I also understood the boomeranging karmic consequences of causing possible harm and inconvenience to another person. No giving myself too hard a time though, that is why I am doing this practice!

Regret

Good, healthy regret. Yes, I regretted making it difficult for the person turning. I don't like it when someone does that to me.

Restraint

I made a plan to stop that harmful habit for a reasonable length of time. I decided to be aware of stopping safely when the lights changed for the rest of my trip to the yoga studio and back. Sounds minor, but it's good to start off with a realistic restraint time (in my case, my trip there and back) instead of something a little more unrealistic like, 'I will never go through a yellow light.'

Recompense

I decided my make-up activity would be to let a motorist into the traffic. I drove the entire way home looking for opportunities to assist until right near the end of the journey I had a chance. The interaction resulted in a friendly wave from them and a big rejoice from me. I had removed an inconsiderate action from my conscience and replaced it with an action of consideration and care toward another. I also consciously tried to feel compassion and forgiveness for myself and the person who tooted at me. Who knows what he had going on?

Rejoice

The Four Forces, especially with the recompense, turned everything around. Instead of letting this incident ruin my day, I happily moved on.

In the scheme of things, running a yellow light may seem minor. But, if we practice with small and niggling inconsiderate actions of body, speech and mind, we learn the wherewithal to work through much bigger difficulties and the serious harms that we or others may cause.

Awareness and healthy regret allows us to move forward free of guilt, blame and victimisation. Making amends makes both our lives, and the lives of others, ever more bearable and beautiful.

The Four Forces can be useful in many scenarios in our lives, let's look at another example next.

How the Four Forces Led to Footy Fun

Using the Four Forces I was able to shift resentment to enjoyment, turning jealousy into real happiness for others.

Have you ever felt resentful, jealous, or even a little unhappy about someone else's happiness? Maybe they landed an amazing job, found a new circle of friends, or set off on an adventure you'd be longing to do.

Or perhaps, as was the case for me, it was something a little more left field. What really pressed my buttons was my husband's absolute devotion to Australian Rules Football. (I'm smiling as I imagine a few fellow 'sport widows' nodding along right now, while the rest of you are shaking your heads).

And while I'm tempted, even now, to feel guilty about my previous anti-footy behaviour, I know that guilt serves no useful purpose. It's also important to acknowledge my feelings and have compassion for the part of myself that felt neglected.

In this case, I managed to shift my resentment to enjoyment!

So let's kick off from here:

Basically, I couldn't understand my husband's passion for football, resenting how much time, joy and focus he devoted to it. I would often make my feelings known in ways subtle and surly, but instead of wallowing in guilt over my past football resentment, I've applied the Four Forces.

This conscience-cleansing exercise is a wonderful way to deal with regrets, past resentments or anything we have done previously that we're not happy about currently.

As previously explained, The Four Forces is predominantly a contemplation in one's own mind, and it may not even be helpful or necessary to tell others what you are doing, so, this is how I applied this practice to my past resentment.

Refuge

Admitting. Yes, I did it: I'd been resentful and jealous, even doing petty, unhelpful things such as ripping a football magazine in half (yes, it's funny looking back on it). Secondly, I knew being like this was not making me happy, and certainly not helping me be the positive force I wanted to be.

Regret

Healthy regret. I am sorry. I behaved unkindly, was envious, and harboured resentment and unhappiness about my husband's football happiness. However, I was doing my best at the time with what I knew and struggled to see I was creating unhappiness. I also didn't see I had alternatives.

Restraint

Awareness. I focussed on the resentment, working kindly with it to restrain myself from making unkind remarks as he prepared to go to games, and I also began to wish him well as he left for matches. A realistic restraint time was important too, so I limited it to when he was preparing to go to matches, rather than making the more unrealistic promise: 'I will never say anything negative about the footy!'

Recompense

Make-up activity. To make amends for past resentment, I'd say a cheerful football goodbye and wish him and Hawthorn (The Hawks) well. I knitted a Hawks beanie too (although the brown and gold colours aren't my favourite combination!) and would make his lunch for matches and help him get tickets for the finals.

Rejoice

Joy. By doing the Four Forces, especially the recompense, I went from feeling (and spreading!) negativity to happy.

This is why the 'Four Forces' exercise is a little like 'mind gardening: most of the work happens in our minds; we are our own judge and jury (there are no footy umpires keeping score!); and the only person we need to satisfy, once we've made amends, is ourselves.

Oh yes, and Go Hawks!

To see how these practices can work together to improve lives, read on.

Awareness, ABCD and The Four Forces, a Combination To Transform Attitudes and Lives

The transformative power of awareness, ABCD, and The Four Forces leads to positivity, connection and frees us to form new habits including embracing happiness for others.

How might the combination of these practices help you? For me they helped me move from a feeling of ill will about others' happiness and the resulting guilt of feeling that ill will. As part of the practice, clearing my conscience also gave me the space to contemplate why I felt so upset and jealous about another person's happiness, in this case, my husband's interest in the football.

By being *aware* of these thought habits, we come to understand that we can change them. We can also examine the effect of our thoughts. For instance, I know it's not helpful for me to be unhappy about someone else's happiness as it just makes me and others miserable.

So, when I am *aware* of these feelings of envy, I now check in with my wise self to question these untrue thoughts and get some helpful advice. Kindly questioning untrue thoughts like: 'He cares more about the football than me'; and 'Football is his number one priority'. I then ask: 'Is this thought helpful to me? Is this thought helping me be happier and more available to others?'

If the thought is not kind, encouraging, or making us available to connect with others, chances are it is not helpful to reinforce or re-live it over and over.

Many years ago I set out to change things around. I applied different practices such as awareness, questioning, ABCD, and the Four Forces. When I was *aware* of the feeling of resentment, I did not push it away, or indulge it either. Instead, I took some Breaths to let the feelings of football unhappiness and resentment pass through, tuned into and Connected with my wise self, and followed up with what to Do—a Four Forces with the recompense to be happy for him and wish him well at the footy. I would, as Lama Marut used to say, 'pile on' to his happiness.

Now, I love it when he heads off to see his Hawks. Fortunately, as I write this, they are doing well, so he usually comes back happy—and I am happier too. I have even reached the point of being able to wash those brown and gold-coloured Hawks socks and boxers with joy.

I am so grateful to many wonderful teachers and friends who have taught me practices like ABCD and the Four Forces to help me transform negative, unhelpful habits, and be a more positive, happy force in the world.

The next chapter extends on these practices with a fun reflection.

Pile onto Other's Happiness

This reflection reminds us of the power of being happy for others who are happy, and being compassionate for those who are not happy.

People being happy for people who are happy—what a magical thing! It's all about encouraging us to let go of envy and instead rejoice in the little things that bring others joy, and though this isn't considered a foundational practice, it feels right at home to include it here.

Lama Marut called being happy for others '*piling on*'—as the players do in rugby when players stream in from all corners of the ground to celebrate by leaping and stacking on top of each other. I love the vision, joy and community the concept of 'piling on' evokes.

I had an opportunity to practice this during the AFL grand final and 'pile on' to the collective joy of my family.

Thank goodness for footy and footy finals! I never thought I'd hear myself say that after years of resentment about (my perception of) others' obsession with football. But now, as footy finals approach again, I too feel the joy it brings to so many around me. Joy that's especially needed here in Melbourne—and everywhere else—after cold winters, pandemics, and other difficult events.

I see people in footy gear, houses decorated, footballs being kicked in parks and cheering fans in stadiums. It reminds me I have a choice: to be a negative stick-in-the-mud, envious of the joy that footy brings, or I can *pile* on to the happy bus.

I'm on the Western Bulldogs bandwagon. Raised in Footscray, Bulldog territory, my Nan went to every home game at the Western Oval to watch the Doggies play, and would scream at the radio during away games. I like to think Nan and I helped to save the Footscray Bulldogs because I donated the $100 she left me in her will to help the club avoid a merger in 1989!

So, it is apt to use the rugby term 'pile on' here: when we are happy for others' happiness, an action that creates an upward spiral of joy for ourselves and others.

Conversely, when we observe unhappiness in ourselves or others, the most helpful response is compassion. It can be tricky to be happy for the winning team if it isn't ours—and just as hard to graciously offer compassion to ourselves or others in defeat—but it's well worth it for the peace of mind it brings.

Our dear dog Maggie, who passed away recently, has had her likeness embroidered on a cushion. I sat with her, in cushion form, on the couch and we watched the Grand Final together. We were ready to pile onto the happiness of the winning team, and to offer compassion to the team and supporters who were defeated.

As it turned out, we needed to show compassion to ourselves and the Doggies team and supporters, while piling onto the joy of the Melbourne Demons and all their fans.

HEART-FRIENDLY WAYS TO PRACTICE

Thank you for reading these reflections and giving your energy to understanding these Foundational Practices.

Here are some ways to practise them when ready.

1. ABCD

Choose something minor that has triggered you: perhaps you too have felt frustrated in traffic; been hurt by a critical or unkind comment; or felt sad about being left out of a social event. Work kindly with yourself and bring awareness to what is going on, then make the most of the ABCD practice:

- **A is for accepting the feeling, thought or situation.** Honour what you are experiencing by holding it lightly, befriending it and feeling it – avoiding suppression, reactive expression or feeding it with blame, criticism, justification or self-depreciating story lines

- **B is for breathing.** Take some breaths into the heart to continue to befriend, feel and gently release the feelings and thoughts. Allow them all to pass through

- **C is connecting** with our wise intuitive selves at the heart and asking for advice on how to respond, for what to do.

- **D is for doing that,** maybe you've been reminded to be kind and encouraging to yourself or others, to forgive, to be happy for someone who has what you want or to be compassionate to another or yourself who is going through difficulty.

2. Four Forces

Choose something minor that you regret doing. I always find it better to start small to build up my Four Forces muscles. Maybe you have said something to someone that you regret; taken something and not returned it; not followed through on a commitment; not picked up your dog's pooh or some rubbish you have seen on a walk; been stingy or judgmental or critical of another or yourself. As you do this practice, remember to be kind to yourself and to make it light and fun.

Do a Four Forces to clear your conscience:

Refuge: Firstly, admit it. Yes, I did it.
Bring understanding and awareness that this thing you regret will be imprinted on your conscience and affect your peace of mind. Don't give yourself a hard time though; that is why you are doing this practice.

Regret: Good healthy regret. Yes, I regret doing it. I don't like it when someone does that to me.

Restraint: Make a plan to stop the harmful habit for a reasonable, realistic length of time

Recompense: Plan a make-up activity to make amends for the misdeed.

Rejoice: Feel really happy about doing these Four Forces, especially about following through on the recompense. Instead of letting this regret ruin your peace of mind, happily move on.

Let's feel glad for all the positive energy we have created together and dedicate this to the happiness and wellbeing of all.

Coming into play in the next section is karma. See you there.

The Four Forces purification practice

1. Lama Marut, *A Spiritual Renegades Guide to the Good Life*, (Atria, Simon and Schuster 2012), Chapter 7, pgs. 198-201

2. Khenchen Konchog Gyaltshen, *A Comprehensive Guide to the Buddhist Path*, (Snowlion 2013).

4. CAUSALITY / KARMA

And The First Three of the Ten Guidelines for a Good Life

CAUSALITY / KARMA

Taking time to understand true causality—or karma as it's commonly called—and how it works, allows us to actively put the true causes into place, not only to sustain our amazing lives, but to create the causes and conditions for lasting peace and happiness. We'll outline how causality is at the heart of ethics and how it works, as well as the first three of the Ten Buddhist Ethical Guidelines (or Ten Guidelines for a Good Life). Knowing the rules related to life enhances our ability to create a happy, well-lived one.

How Our Actions Echo Through Our Lives

As a parent, I often said, 'Good things happen to those who do good.' As I've explored teachings on karma more deeply, I've come to understand the threads of causality beneath that simple phrase and how they shape a more intentional life.

When my children were young and in response to a Duplo train set war or similar dispute, I would often say, 'Good things happen to those who do good'. I understood little about causality, or about 'karma', as it is known in the Indo-Tibetan traditions. But I knew enough to understand that it always felt better to try to do the kind thing. And it felt like a helpful thing to teach the kids, as well as to hear myself say too.

I've been very thankful to study and learn more about karma or causality from my teachers. In his book, *'A Spiritual Renegade's Guide to the Good Life'*, [1] Lama Marut teaches how to create and sustain happiness in our complex modern age. He offers practical and honest advice, and I continue to do my best to put this wisdom into practice in everyday life. Lama Marut's book and the guidance I received from my teachers in the Tibetan and Yoga traditions inspire much of what I share here.

In studying karma or cause and effect, we're invited to contemplate why things happen. There are three possible explanations: **The first is that things happen randomly, for no reason at all;** it's just good luck or bad luck. This viewpoint gives us no control at all: we are just victims of things happening randomly to us and around us. However, we like to believe this is true when bad things happen—like having an accident—because if we believe it's just random bad luck, we don't need to take any responsibility for it.

The second possibility is that there is some external God micromanaging everything. If we believe in this micromanaging God, again, we have no control over what is happening to us, as everything is 'God's will'. In my experience this does not mitigate having a relationship with a divine principal in our lives—like when I check in with my wise, intuitive self—but it removes the idea that we are entirely at the mercy of external forces. Checking in with my internal, wise, intuitive self for how to respond to what is going on gives me agency to take responsibility and act from wisdom.

The third, and only plausible explanation for why things happen is the karmic or causality worldview: a deeper truth behind how things happen.

Karma is often misunderstood. For instance, it can be incorrectly associated with the idea of fate—when we believe, for instance, that misfortune is our lot in life. This misunderstanding (as with the ideas of things happening randomly or a micromanaging God) makes us victims of what is going on. It assumes there is nothing we can do about it.

When we understand Karma or causality, we can take full responsibility for our lives and how we live them, knowing that our actions matter. Because within each choice we make, we can either generate positive karma that will move us toward well-being through acts of kindness and generosity, or conversely, we create the experience of unhappiness through harmful or greedy behaviour.

Becoming clear on how cause and effect play out in our lives is a long-term project, but we can start now by integrating the 'golden and silver rules', wonderful guidelines to live by and which we explore next.

The Golden and Silver Rules

The secrets of karma can be understood through the Golden and Silver Rules. In further discussing causality, we explore the karmic delivery system, empowering conscious, responsible living.

The concept of karma and causality is reflected in the Golden and Silver rules and the saying 'What goes around, comes around'. I tend to think of it as: what we give out, comes back to us, just like a boomerang.

The Golden Rule:
Do unto others as you would have them do unto you.

The 'unto' used to throw me for a bit of a loop. I simply like to remember to treat others as I would like to be treated: kindly.

The Silver Rule:
Do not do unto others as you would not want them to do unto you.

Again, the 'unto'! I simply like to remember not to treat others as I would not like them to treat me: unkindly.

I've spent much time examining my motivations for trying to live by these guidelines. Motivation to be a 'good girl' (to please an authoritarian figure) is different from a genuine wish to connect with others through kindness. For example, if I refrain from saying something to prevent harm because I want to appear 'nice' and for others to like me, my motivation and action need a gentle rethink.

Taking time to further understand true causality is worth the effort. While we might have a surface understanding of how causality works, some deeper insights are worth considering. For example, we may think that a good diet and exercise are the 'true' causes for good health, yet some people who lead healthy lives end up getting ill, contracting diseases, and dying young. So, let's explore further to understand causality and the true nature of a cause.

A cause has to be present for an effect to arise, and every effect naturally leads to some result. If there's no true cause in place, the effect can't appear.

Using the healthy-lifestyle example: if living healthily were the *real* cause of a long life, then everyone who ate well, exercised and looked after themselves would *always* enjoy a long, healthy life. But we know that's not how life works.

So, the 'cause and effect' we usually assume must be more complex than it appears. Our everyday idea of causality can't fully explain what's actually happening.

We need to understand associative conditions and how they relate to causality. Using the example above, the conditions for good health might be seen as leading a healthy lifestyle, eating well, and exercising. These are the associative conditions that allow the 'true causes' for things to be expressed. Lama Marut refers to these as the 'karmic delivery system'.[2]

Exercising and eating well are two possible delivery systems for good health, but if we haven't created the actual 'causes' for good health, we won't experience good health no matter how hard we exercise or eat well.

So how do we create the karma for experiencing good health?

The teachings I've received suggest the true cause for good health is protecting and caring for the life of others. If we do this, we are creating the causes for the conditions of exercising and eating well to deliver us good health.

Holding this view of true causality and how it relates to the karmic delivery system allows us to take responsibility for putting the causes in place for the life we want. We will explore ways to integrate or 'home-bake' these understandings into our lives throughout this book.

What Goes Around Comes Around

When exploring the essence of karma, 'What goes around comes around', every action matters and shapes our experiences. Navigating causality reveals timeless truths.

I like to think of karma or causality as 'What goes around comes around.' Everything matters: whatever we do, say, or think. I find the analogy of planting a seed and its ripening into a sprout useful here. The so-called 'good' things (like practicing generosity, kindness and the desire to help others) will plant a seed in our mind which, in time, will sprout into our experiencing a positive effect. However, both the form the experience takes and the time it will arise are unknown.

Conversely, doing so-called 'bad' things (like being greedy, wanting to harm, or indulging in unhealthy pride) plants a seed that will ripen into our experiencing negative results. Again, the form and timing unknown.

As we have discussed, holding a karmic worldview can be tricky because we can be fooled by false causality, such as when it seems the causes for good health come only from diet and exercise. We know, however, that can't be the way things work because if exercise were the true cause of good health, then everyone who exercised would always be healthy. Using the seed-planning analogy, the deeper cause of good health would be the past karmic seeds we've planted, such as contributing to the health of others. Then, when we do eat well and exercise, these become the delivery system for experiencing our own good health.

That said, I once enthusiastically embarked on a healthy eating plan, only to become sick! Clearly, I had not put the deeper causes in place for my healthy eating plan to be the delivery system for feeling strong and well.

Like most of us, I like to take credit for the great things that happen to me, but I am often reluctant to take responsibility for the not-so-great things. Still, I try to remember that causality is always at play. An example I like to use is when someone huffs at me when I fumble for my payment card at the supermarket. What goes around comes around, so no doubt I have been impatient myself in the past! That huff is the delivery system for the past karmic seed of impatience I previously planted. I know that is true, even though often, I don't want to admit it!

So, what is my best response here? To be patient, and not huff back, so as not to create the cause for more future impatience.

I also try not to bash myself up for past mistakes! Back when I was impatient with others I was doing my best with what I knew at the time and now I have an opportunity to do my best with more information and understanding. So, no huffing back. And no beating myself up for past impatience either. My best response? Admit it, and do a Four Forces, the making amends or conscience-clearing practice we discussed in Section 3.

The causality time gap:

Another way we are deceived by false causality is forgetting that there is a *causality time gap.* While cause and effect are always at play, there isn't always a direct cause and effect relationship between two things that appear connected in the moment. Sometimes, we do a 'good' thing—like smiling at someone—and they give us a frown back. This can throw us for a loop and cause us to question causality, but remember, there's a time gap between cause and effect.

That's right, there's no direct causal link between a kind action, giving a smile, and an unkind response, receiving a frown. The kind smile we offered will have its positive result, but maybe not straight away. The unkind experience of a frown, however, is a 'what goes around comes around' too: it results from a past unkindness on our behalf.

Once we build up more seeds of kindness, receiving a frown may even elicit a feeling of compassion in us rather than a feeling of unkindness. And as we've learned, karma is always at play. So, we *will* receive a good result from our smile, we just don't know in what form or when. As it says at Armadale railway station, and it always makes me smile: 'Mind the (causality time) Gap'.

All aboard for the next chapter where we'll explore this on a deeper level.

If all this is a bit much for now, all you really need to remember is: do good, or simply be kind, because doing good or being kind is the right, wise thing to do—and it feels good too.

The Karma Cam is Always On

Here we'll explore the four laws of karma through a practical, down-to-earth lens.

Sometimes, when we learn a bit about causality, it's tempting to think it means we can control our lives, what happens to us and get exactly what we want by manipulating karma. Spoiler alert: this is not the case. Causality is always at play. The karma cam always on.

How karma works is not fathomable. The workings of karma are considered 'deeply hidden' and unknowable, and that's also the beauty of it—not knowing exactly when karma kicks in is what makes life so fun and interesting!

What we have more control over though is *how* we respond to 'what comes around'. In my example of being huffed impatiently at the supermarket, I can be confident that my response will plant a nice new calm and patient seed in my mind. In the future, I will experience it back in some form; I just don't know how, where, or when.

There are four so-called laws or principles of karma:

1. **Our actions are definite and certain to result in similar consequences.**

2. **Karma grows: The effect that we create, either positive or negative, will be greater than the cause. So, a small deed of kindness will come back to us**

as a bigger deed of kindness and vice-versa; even a small unkindness will grow into us experiencing greater unpleasantness in the future.

3. A positive action with the intention of kindness will always produce a positive result and never a negative one.

4. Conversely, a negative action intended to harm will always produce a negative result and never a positive one.

Looking at this a little closer, there can be no effect without a cause. If we do nothing to create a cause, then we will never experience the corresponding result.

Similarly, there can be no cause without an effect. Once we're created a cause for something, we will experience the result, unless it is mitigated by our conscious practice of the Four Forces.

Karma also tends to grow. The effect we create, either positive or negative, will be greater than the cause if we do nothing to rectify our behaviour, or especially if we revel in hurting another.

In these reflections, we're not focusing solely on external events, but mostly exploring mental karma which is how our thoughts, intentions and actions shape our inner experience and perception of our lives and how things are unfolding. When misfortune does arrive, it's never helpful to blame or criticise ourselves or others, especially as we are all doing the best we know at the time.

Doing good, because doing good is the right thing to do, is 'instant karma' in a way. Often, when we do good, it feels great too. How I see myself act, think, and speak in the world shapes the perception I have of myself. So, if I see myself acting as a positive, considerate, kind force in the world, I will have that perception of myself. Which is a much nicer head to live in and a better internal soundtrack to listen to than the opposite!

True causality is at the heart of ethics. 'Doing good' means living according to ethical guidelines that we feel benefit our own happiness and the happiness of others. The laws of karma help us understand the real reason it's important to live an ethical life and encourage us to stay aware of our intention, and to continue to hold this view, even when deceived by how things appear on the surface.

With karma and its correlations at its heart, next we'll look at some guidelines for creating a good life based on ethical behaviour.

Again - if this feels a bit much for now, all you really need to remember is: do good, or simply be kind, because doing good or being kind is the right, wise thing to do—and it feels good too.

Ten Guidelines for a Good Life

Living by ethical guidelines and taking time for reflection can shape our lives and bring peace.

In Buddhism, just as in other religious traditions, there are ethical guidelines. And just like in many such traditions, they are ten in number. In Islam they're called the Ten Obligatory Acts, and in Christianity, the Ten Commandments. I was brought up with the Ten Commandments which I must admit I had little understanding of, or resonance with. Buddhist studies introduced me to the Ten Misdeeds (also called the Ten Non-Virtuous Actions) which, as explained to me, have become a very helpful way to navigate life. Causality is at the heart of these guidelines, along with the karmic correlations associated with each of the misdeeds.

Misdeeds are basically harmful or unhelpful acts that disturb the lives and inner peace of both ourselves and others. They can relate to actions of our body, speech, and mind.

The Ten Misdeeds to be avoided, and their positive opposites, help us better understand life, in terms of what's beneficial and what's detrimental. These ethical guidelines represent a universal code of behaviour, offering us a handbook for life to help us avoid major undesirable future worries, while creating more contentment and peace.

I will word them as Lama Marut taught and presented them in his book, *A Spiritual Renegades Guide to the Good Life.*[3]

The three related to the body are:

- harming ourselves or others
- stealing
- disrespecting relationships

The four related to speech are:

- harsh speech
- meaningless speech
- speech that excludes others
- untruthful speech.

The last three related to the mind are:

- being unhappy when others are happy
- being happy when others are unhappy
- holding incorrect world views

We can often resist ethical guidelines because we don't like being told what and what not to do. But it helps to understand why it's in our best interest to apply these to the way we live. To do that, it's helpful to dig a little deeper into karma or causality—which is the reason ethical behaviour matters.

As outlined earlier, karma can be thought of simply as, 'what goes around comes around'. So, if we put positive deeds of body, speech and mind into the world, we can experience them coming back to us. And the opposite is also true, in that when we act harmfully, it too will boomerang back. Understanding this can motivate us to avoid creating negative karmic causes. It also offers us guidance on how to create positive causes for the life we want to build.

Simply put, these ten ethical guidelines are designed to help us reduce the suffering and increase the happiness of ourselves and others by living a life of kindness and compassion.

Here is the list of The Ten Guidelines, as presented in *'The Spiritual Renegades Guide to the Good Life'.*

---

1. **Don't kill**—protect and honour life
2. **Don't steal**—treat other people's things with respect and practice generosity
3. **Don't hurt others with your sexual activity**—respect and foster others' relationships
4. **Don't lie**—tell the truth
5. **Don't use your word to drive a wedge between people**—speak in ways to bring people together
6. **Don't hurt people with your words**—use words that are kind and pleasing to others
7. **Don't engage in useless speech**—make your words meaningful and sincere
8. **Don't be envious of other people's lives**—rejoice in the little things that bring pleasure to others
9. **Don't be happy about other people's pain and problems**—be compassionate and empathic
10. **Don't adhere to erroneous views**—adopt viewpoints that are correct

In the next chapters, we'll reflect on the first three of these in more detail.

Guideline One: Protect and Honour Life

These ethical guidelines can help us align more closely with our values and live with greater meaning. Many people, myself included, find them incredibly helpful.

The first three ethical guidelines relate to actions of the body. Here's the first as I have learned and practiced it:

Don't kill—protect and honour life:

This is about practicing non-violence and not physically harming others. It refers to protecting all life, even that of small insects, what we often call 'pests' or bugs. When it comes to death, sickness, or physical pain of any sort, we can observe that all living beings want to avoid it, and have the right to do so. So why would we want to harm others—and our current and future selves—by doing what we all most fear: harm?

If we want to feel protected and honoured in our own lives, we need to practice protecting and honouring the lives of all living beings, including ourselves. This can look like being kind and encouraging, as well as taking care of your health and well-being so you can be in good shape to also benefit others. For me, this has included mental health too, so being aware of my harsh, critical inner voice and replacing it with a kind and encouraging one, by tuning into and listening to my wise self for truth and guidance.

Although complete non-violence is an ideal (as it's impossible to exist without causing some type of harm), it's humbling to realise that our very existence causes harm to others, often without being conscious of it. For instance, we kill insects on our windscreens during a road trip (let alone the damage caused in the creation of the vehicle and extraction of the fuel that powers it); and even non-drivers may harm the habitat of bugs while trying to create a beautiful garden. What's important though is our *intention* to practice non-harm: respecting and caring for the lives of others as best we can.

Many Buddhist and Yogic texts outline the karmic correlations to practicing non-harm. Among the positive correlations are experiencing good health and longevity. And among the negative ones are physical health issues. Many spiritual leaders such as the Dalai Lama and Gandhi emphasise practising non-harm by respecting and caring for others, not only for their welfare but for the welfare of our future selves.

If practising non-harm is about how we treat people, the next guideline gently extends that care to how we treat the belongings of others.

Guideline Two: Respect Others' Things and Practice Generosity

The second of the ethical guidelines related to the body is about not taking what doesn't belong to us.

Don't steal—treat other people's things with respect and practice generosity:

I can still picture it clearly. I was about seven years old and shopping with my mother at Sims Supermarket, Footscray. Right at child-height a hook dangled a brightly coloured, tastebud tempting packet of jelly. I'm not sure now if I'd confused it with some other samples, or had intentionally stolen it, but when my mother discovered it, she facilitated a rather forceful Four Forces, marching me back to the supermarket, demanding I apologise, and return the jelly. It was, and remains, a valuable lesson.

Decades later I can remember the a-ha moment when I learnt about the all-inclusive nature of stealing. Lama Marut taught me that stealing means taking anything that does not belong to you. There is stealing that is obvious, including shop-lifting and taking things without asking, but what I hadn't stopped to consider was that stealing also included things like: making personal calls when working, not returning loaned items promptly, stringing out paying back debts, 'borrowing' office supplies from work, unnecessarily taking up people's time, or even snacking on a marshmallow at the Mission kitchen—a small crime I committed while at work (although I conducted a Four Forces, and replaced the marshmallows).

I was also made aware that on a more macro level, we are stealing from others when we consume more of the world's resources than we actually need, meaning that present and future generations might not have enough fresh water, top soil, or energy. A Gandhi recommendation that comes to mind is, to live simply so others can simply live.

Reflecting on karmic correlations, we can again see the truth behind the phrase 'what goes around comes around,' in that when we take what doesn't belong to us, we plant the seeds to experience loss ourselves.

Lama Marut used to say, 'The Karma Cam is always on!' Meaning, if we observe ourselves performing acts of stealing, those acts imprint on our conscience and can result in a perceived or real lack of material things like resources, money, food and shelter.

Alternatively, respecting other people's belongings and practicing generosity ensures we feel we have enough. These are the positive correlations to the guideline of not stealing. By being respectful and generous, we create the real and perceived causes to experience abundance and sufficiency.

Respect doesn't stop with people or possessions it also shows up in how we honour the relationships in our lives, which is what the next chapter covers.

Guideline Three: Respect and Foster Connections

The third of the Ten Buddhist Misdeeds relates to understanding boundaries in order to foster better relationships. This reminder promotes truthful and respectful behaviour with others.

Following on from the first two misdeeds, the third focuses on our intentions and behaviour regarding our relationships, specifically adultery.

The third misdeed is:

Don't hurt others with your sexual activity—respect and foster others' relationships.

Lama Marut explains that, 'Adultery means having sexual relations with someone other than your partner (assuming you have mutually agreed not too) or, if single with someone who is married or otherwise seriously and exclusively committed to another.' [4]

Adultery hurts people in many ways, including through the betrayal of trust. Texts I've studied refer to other potential future consequences including: unfaithful spouses; others trying to form a relationship with your partner; people around you such as friends family and workmates seeming untrustworthy; perceiving others as enemies; and perceiving our environment as dirty and polluted.

So, if we want a sexual partner and others in our lives we can trust, a nice clean environment and to be surrounded by friendly people, we need to refrain from hurting others through our sexual activity.

This puts the causes in place for a positive future. We can do this by respecting others' relationships (respecting others in general is a great practice!) and supporting others' relationships. For me, this includes doing my best to refrain from harmful gossip about others and not passing unhelpful judgment on others or their relationships. Like many people, I find it hard to not put my two cents in about how others behave in relationships, but it's helpful to remember to judge the behaviour, not the person, while understanding we do not know what is going on for others. Compassion for all, including ourselves, is much more helpful than conjecture, judgment and blame.

Instead, we can be complimentary of others when we see good things going on, and do what we can to promote understanding, care, compassion, and respect in all relationships.

> **The following five relationship guidelines are good reminders for all partners of this:**
> stay faithful; make them feel wanted; respect your partner; don't flirt with others; and make time for them.

Remember, we are human, and at times we may behave in ways which are disrespectful or harmful to others or their relationships. When this happens, rather than blaming or victimising yourself or others, take responsibility for the misbehaviour, and do the trusty Four Forces practice to make amends and create peace of mind.

HEART-FRIENDLY WAYS TO PRACTICE

Thank you for sharing your time, heart and headspace in this section.

Let's close by putting a new habit in place.

You may like to:

- Choose one habit related to harm that you would like to change - start small.
- Maybe you would like to develop the intention to not kill insects or rodents by catching bugs in a jar and putting them outside, storing food in sealed containers or using an ethical mouse trap.
- Be mindful of the all-inclusive nature of stealing and make an effort to respect others things and time.
- Be aware of not joining in harmful gossip related to others partners and relationships.
- Be on the look out for critical self-talk and replace it with kind encouragement.
- Perhaps practice that crucial, uplifting view now: rejoice that we've tackled and contemplated this challenging material – good for us!
- Take three mindful breaths and think about the good energy we have created by contemplating, reviewing and implementing these helpful practices.
- Let's rejoice in that. Dedicate that positive energy towards the happiness and wellbeing of others and yourself.

Let's feel glad for all the positive energy we have created together and dedicate this to the happiness and wellbeing of all.

Having explored causality and the first three guidelines, we can now move into the next set—the ones that shape our speech and our inner world.

How to live a good life

1. Lama Marut, *A Spiritual Renegades Guide to the Good Life*, (Atria, Simon and Schuster 2012). Introduction.

The Karmic delivery system

2. Lama Marut, *A Spiritual Renegades Guide to the Good Life*, (Atria, Simon and Schuster 2012), Chapter 3, p.47.

The Ten misdeeds

3. Lama Marut, *A Spiritual Renegades Guide to the Good Life*, (Atria, Simon and Schuster 2012), Chapter 7, pgs.180-196.

4. Lama Marut, *A Spiritual Renegades Guide to the Good Life*, (Atria, Simon and Schuster 2012), Chapter 7, p.186.

5. TEN GUIDELINES FOR A GOOD LIFE

The Seven Related to Speech and Mind

Ten Guidelines for a Good Life: The Seven Related to Speech and Mind.

We've explored causality and the first three of the Ten Buddhist Ethical Guidelines, now we'll look more closely at the next seven. Understanding and practicing the four related to speech and the three related to our mind will promote contentment and peace of mind, assisting us in creating and sustaining the causes for a good life.

Guideline Four: Truthfulness

The fourth misdeed relates to lying, and ensuring the truth is told.

The first of the four misdeeds relating to our speech is about being truthful and not lying. In yoga, these relate to our throat chakra or Vishuddhi chakra. A chakra can be thought of as an energy centre. In my POM Yoga sessions, we enjoy a chakra-based practice to clear the ignorant energy at the different chakras. This encourages the energy of wisdom to flow freely, so we know what to say, to whom, and when. When working with my Vishuddhi chakra, I always remind myself to let go of any unhelpful speech. That means speech not truthful, inclusive, kind and meaningful.

I also to try to be aware of my internal dialogue, checking in with my wise self to replace any untrue, critical, unkind thoughts with positive, kind, encouraging ones. We'll share more about that in the upcoming reflections.

So yes, the first of the four misdeeds related to speech is:

Don't lie—tell the truth:

I can be thankful to my mother for instilling this in me throughout my life. Honesty was her big thing, and she had no hesitation calling us kids out when we were loose with the facts. She was right, being dishonest can get us into lots of strife, as I was reminded recently by watching *Bridget Jones's Baby* [1] with the 'Who is the father?' debacle; as well as the old saying 'Liar, Liar Pants on Fire'; and of course Aesop's Fable *The Boy Who Cried Wolf.* [2]

However, as I studied this misdeed more deeply, it crystallised for me that lying means giving someone an impression different from the one that you actually have. This definition means that if we think something is one way and we give a different representation of the situation to someone else, then we are lying.

One morning I recalled this when I caught myself about to give someone a different impression to what I was truly experiencing. I was in Maggie Island, Queensland, spending some time writing, reading and relaxing. It was beautiful and the heat and humidity didn't bother me. What I was about to tell my friend on the phone though (who was in cold Melbourne and going through a tricky time), was that it was hot, steamy, and uncomfortable.

When I questioned myself as to why I was tempted to lie, I realised it was probably about feeling a little guilty about being there, doing what I was doing. I was reminded of something I heard Lama Marut teach: just because you have something good (a lovely, relaxing break away) does not mean that you are preventing someone else from having it, too. So, I decided to be grateful for the break, enjoy it, and dedicate my happiness and good fortune toward my friend's happiness in the future.

With that thought in mind, I notice I'm tempted to lie when I don't want to hurt people's feelings by telling the truth. While it's not good karmically to hurt people's feelings with negative (but true) comments, it's also not good to lie—so what do we do? We employ skilful means, which is an artful dance between the two.

I remember Lama Marut encouraging us to be creative about finding something truthfully positive to say about something we don't like. This avoids hurting someone's feelings. His example of how to respond to, 'How do you like my purple polka dot, polyester dress?' always sticks in my mind. I can hear him saying, 'You can always find something nice and truthful to say about the damned dress.' His suggestions include, 'It fits well', or 'I like the purple colour', or even 'You got it for a great price'. Checking in with our wise selves for what to say is always helpful.

Giving someone a false impression of what is *really* going on though means we are imprinting our consciousness negatively. The karmic consequence of lying is that we will have the perception of being lied to by others. This makes us feel ever more uneasy, distrustful and alone. In addition, we will experience others not believing us, even when we are telling the truth. If, however, we are truthful; we experience others as trusting what we say and being truthful with us too. Bliss!

Unfortunately, our internal speech and thoughts can also lie to us, so being aware of harmful internal dialogue, questioning its truth, and replacing it with positive, kind, and encouraging words is a very worthwhile practice for our peace of mind. I practice this by being *aware* of the emotion triggered or harmful dialogue, followed by an ABCD to Connect with the wise intuitive energy at the heart for guidance, which often involves giving myself the kind encouragement I need.

Remember that we are human, and at times will behave in untruthful ways. When this happens, rather than using blame or victimisation of ourselves and others, we can take responsibility for our mistake and do our Four Forces practice to make amends, heal, connect and create peace of mind.

Forgive yourself and others, and be kind and encouraging to all with your speech—that is the way to go.

What makes me so happy though is knowing that beyond avoiding harm, our speech also has the power to bring people together, so we'll explore that next.

Guideline Five: Bringing People Together

Let's explore the second misdeed related to speech, number five on our list of the Ten Misdeeds. It advises us not to use words to drive wedges.

When emotions are running high, it's easy to express ourselves in unhelpful ways. However, pausing to connect with wise speech can help us respond more thoughtfully. So, before we dive in to Guideline Five, I'd like to share a few questions I find helpful to ask myself before I speak:

1. **Is it true?** Or is it exaggerated? Watch out for using words like *always* and *never*, as these often point to untruths and exaggerations.
2. **Is it out of context?** For example, it may not be appropriate to discuss political concerns at a child's birthday party.
3. **Is it well-intended and kind?** Consider your motivation. Why are you saying this? Is it genuinely helpful and kind?
4. **Is it necessary?** Do I really need to say this?
5. **Is it timely?** Is this the right time to be discussing this?

This little checklist often helps me decide whether a tricky conversation is worth having, or whether it would be better for me just to let it go.

Okay, so let's discuss, Vishuddi, or our throat chakra, which relates to speech and the four misdeeds related to it. The second of these four is:

Don't use your words to drive a wedge between people —speak in ways that bring people together.

Divisive speech is when we say something about someone, to someone else, intending to create division. I can recall doing this as a teenager, when I had the misguided idea that turning someone against another person would somehow make me more popular.

Of course, the reverse was true.

The karmic correlation related to this kind of speech is that we lose friends quickly, we experience others as speaking badly of us, and we perceive conflict around us. Another karmic correlation I found curious is that we may also perceive ourselves living in an environment where travel becomes difficult. Lama Marut explained that by tearing others apart through our words, we may create the karmic causes for experiencing difficulty in joining ourselves to our destination.

Instead of being divisive, we can use our speech to bring others together. We can say nice things about others, especially when they are not around. We have many opportunities to be inclusive, and it always feels good. Many years ago, I had the opportunity to do so when I introduced a new mother, Pip, at my children's primary school to the other mums. She still reminds me how included it made her feel, and we are good friends to this day, some thirty years later.

It's not surprising that by being inclusive with our speech, we generate loyal friends and more harmonious relationships in the future.

From here we can develop even more skills regarding how we use our words.

Guideline Six: Kind and Pleasing Words

The third misdeed relating to speech is about being selective with our words in order to be kind and pleasing towards others—i.e.: don't hurt people with your words!

Checking in with my wise self before speaking and aiming for words that are kind and encouraging helps me align with the third, of the four misdeeds relating to speech:

Don't hurt people with your words—use words that are kind and pleasing to others.

Harsh speech includes words that hurt others. It also can affect us, if our internal dialogue is unkind. Awareness of such unkind internal speech, and replacing it with kind encouraging words, is a meaningful practice that gives peace of mind. Practicing kind speech, both to ourselves and others, is life-changing.

Whether we're speaking to ourselves or others, it's our *intention* that matters more than what we say or how we say it. Harsh speech can be loud, full of swearing or sarcasm, or even soft and sweet. It is considered harsh speech though if the intention behind it is to hurt.

The karmic correlation for speaking harshly is that we will perceive others as speaking unkindly to us, and saying things we don't want to hear. Have you ever had times in your life where you're constantly perceiving people as difficult or argumentative?

I have! Being aware of kind speech helps us avoid creating the causes for such perceptions.

Another karmic correlation for harsh speech is the perception of noise pollution. Until we refrain from harsh speech, we will experience our environment as being disturbed by unpleasant noise. The teachings suggest that to avoid all types of unwanted noises—including people criticising or abusing us, and noisy neighbours—we can try to create a harmonious environment around us. This can be done by using kind, friendly, and pleasant speech, both externally and internally.

With regard to our internal speech—the little and sometimes loud voice in our head—rather than listen to a harsh, critical internal soundtrack, we have the power to play a different tune featuring kind, encouraging words. The lyrics of Helen Reddy's song, *Best Friend* [3] remind me of this. The words suggest if we realised we were our own best friends we would take better care of ourselves and be kinder and more forgiving of our humanness.

Helen tells us this best-friend self is always with us, on our side and there to make sure we get our share and are treated fairly. This friend will never let us down. Her words encourage me to be my own best friend. And as part of that I'm reminded how, before communicating, it's so helpful to check-in with my wise self or best-friend self for kind and encouraging suggestions. An ABCD practice is always useful for this.

In the yoga practice I lead, when we meditate on the throat chakra, I encourage us to check in with our wise selves by taking a Breath and Connecting with our deep intuitive wisdom at the heart. Here we listen for some words which are kind and encouraging, and say these words to ourselves three times. It might be nice to try for yourself.

In Buddhism, there is a practice called the Four Immeasurables, and these can be thought of as ways to act toward ourselves and others: with Loving Kindness or Friendliness; Compassion; Sympathetic Joy; and Equanimity.

The first of these, Loving Kindness and Friendliness, is inherent in our internal speech to ourselves and external speech to others. I love the word 'friendly' and how it feels to have friends and to be a friend to others and ourselves too. Being kind and friendly creates the causes for a pleasing and friendly external environment—and internal one too.

And in the moment, kindness and friendliness are their own reward.

In the next chapter, we'll take a look at how sincerity in our words matters too.

Guideline Seven: Meaningful and Sincere Words

We are now up to the fourth and final misdeed relating to speech. Speaking words that are meaningful and sincere makes a positive difference.

Don't engage in useless speech—make your words meaningful and sincere

---

I've taken this guideline to heart, so rather than mess around with any useless words here, let's get straight into these simple guidelines.

Below you might recognise some ways meaningless, idle, or useless speech plays out around you:

Meaningless discussion or debate about things you don't really understand

This could include debating politics or sport without having the background to contribute meaningfully. Certainly, for me, it would be meaningless to discuss at more than a superficial level AFL or in-depth politics!

Speaking for the sake of speaking

Chatting about things that are not meaningful or relevant to others is another way we can waste our words or force them on others. Endlessly discussing food, property, pets or other interests with someone who is not interested wastes everyone's precious time.

Gossiping

This involves idle talk about others and is often more focused on their problems than the good stuff that is happening for them. If you want to talk about other people at all, talk about their positive traits and rejoice in their good fortune! Be aware of the temptation to gossip, it's destructive to your own ability to communicate, be heard, and be respected, and it's also hurtful to the person being talked about. Instead, practice using your speech in ways that are meaningful and sincere.

Saying we will do something and not following through

For example, saying, 'We must catch up soon' when we have no real intention of doing so. By expressing this without sincerity, we hear ourselves say something that is not in line with our true thoughts. As we'll see with karmic correlations: we hear ourselves talking rubbish, and then we come to think of ourselves as rubbish.

The karmic, 'what goes around comes around' consequence of meaningless speech is that no one pays attention to what we say. If we've regularly engaged in idle or insincere speech, people will perceive our words as meaningless, even if we have something of value to say. And because we have not valued our own speech, others will not value it either.

I was struck by a teaching Lama Marut gave about meaningless speech. He suggested that when we constantly hear ourselves 'talking rubbish'—meaningless speech which is not respectful, or making promises we have no intention of following through on—we start to perceive ourselves as having diminished value or worth. It was helpful for me to consider that my lack of confidence, feelings of depression, or low self-esteem could be related to the quality of my speech. Becoming more mindful of my words has greatly benefitted my sense of self-worth.

On the optimistic side of things, there are positive karmic consequences for making our words meaningful and sincere, and ensuring we do what we say we will do. By hearing ourselves speak meaningfully, we begin to see ourselves as someone who is sincere and trustworthy, who follows through and is respectful. Others will sense this too and will be more likely to respect, listen to, and value our contributions.

We can contribute to better relationships too by being happy for others, Guideline Eight on this topic is coming right up.

Guideline Eight: Rejoicing and Happiness!

In expanding the concept of motherhood, we see we're all creators in some way—capable of showing 'motherly' care to ourselves and others through kindness, support and compassion.

The ancient Sufi sage and poet Rumi says, 'Your heart knows the way, run in that direction'. [4] I love that quote, but, as we're all a work in progress, I also acknowledge that sometimes we need to walk before we run. Helping me pick up speed though have been the guidelines on thought shared below.

Don't be envious of other people's lives—rejoice in the little things that bring pleasure to others:

When we're envious of other people, we feel unhappy because they possess something we don't. This is an unhelpful, illogical and ultimately ignorant way to relate to the happiness or success of others. It's illogical because another person's happiness or success—such as them receiving a windfall or enjoying an exciting experience—does not come at the expense of you not receiving the same. Causality is at play: people get desirable things because they have created the causes (or karma) for such good fortune. We just haven't created the causes for that exact thing to happen for ourselves.

We can be thrown for a loop however by false causality. This is when we perceive someone having something desirable, like a new car, after stealing money. These two events may seem related, but causality explains they can't be. The karma for the new car comes from a kind generous deed previously done (who knows when). And the karma associated with stealing is ticking away in the background, the consequences of stealing to be received in the future. It makes logical sense to be happy for those who have created the causes for good fortune while showing compassion to those who have created misfortune through harm and ignorance.

Being happy for others when they have good fortune is the practice of 'sympathetic joy' in the Buddhist tradition. Lama Marut would encourage us to, 'pile onto others' happiness', much like a pile-on celebration in football. Feeling sympathetic joy is beneficial for our own mental and emotional well-being, and it contributes to the happiness of others too.

Alternatively, when we feel *unhappy* about another person's good fortune, that envy is basically a form of greedy discontentment. The karmic result of this is the perception that we never have enough, leaving us feeling discontented. For example, if we are envious of someone else's good looks, we will create the perception that we are not attractive ourselves.

Of course, sometimes it's tricky to feel happy for others. As human beings, we've all felt envy, greed or jealousy. Sometimes, when we hear good news from others, even those we love, we can feel a twinge of envy, anger, or disappointment that it is not us having a win. That's totally normal and certainly not a reason to give ourselves a hard time. Recognising that envy and greed get in the way of expressing sympathetic joy allows us to notice these difficult emotions and work skilfully with them.

Let's take feeling envious of what someone has as an example. When we are aware of the feeling of envy and its associated thoughts, we can do an ABCD for a more helpful way to think.

Wise truths like: 'I have enough', or 'I am content with what I have', and 'I choose to be happy for them', are some we can practice.

Contentment and joy in others' happiness are the opposite of envy. By reacting this way, the bonus is that we create the causes to receive them ourselves. In addition, it's simply a much more enjoyable and fun way to live! As my friend Michelle reminds me: 'We rise by lifting others'.

My life has certainly been lifted by this guideline and the one in the next chapter too See you there!

Guideline Nine: Compassion and Empathy

Now for the ninth guideline to help us live a good life. This one relates to finding compassion and empathy for others, rather than rejoicing in their pain.

The second misdeed relating to our mind is about ill will:

Don't be happy about other people's pain or problems—be compassionate and empathetic.

Have you ever felt happiness about someone else's misfortune? Hoped others experience difficulties? Wanted enemies to suffer or were happy when they did?

Or perhaps you've been pleased when someone you were in competition with failed. Or were entertained by watching, listening to or reading about others' suffering; perhaps taken an interest in others' misfortune, like gawking at car accidents?

These examples of ill will are not only an unhelpful way to think but will also bring further difficulties down the track. When we tune into our wise self and choose self-awareness over ignorance, compassion and empathy are far more likely to arise in our future.

Texts on karmic effects of ill will say because we have wished others harm that harm and a fear of harm comes to us and we can develop a personality dominated by anger, sadistic tendencies and paranoia. That doesn't sound like a nice way to live!

I'll admit it can be tricky at times not to feel just a little bit satisfied when someone we find difficult—or who has harmed us (or others!) —experiences misfortune. We're humans and we all have the capacity to feel ill-will. That's normal, and not a reason to beat ourselves up.

Remembering our Four Forces practice helps us be less judgemental about these emotions, but we can still be discerning, recognising that ill will causes problems for us and can get in the way of our empathy and compassion. Those very qualities, empathy and compassion, help us become ever more aware of how destructive ill-will can be, and lead us to more skilful ways to behave and respond.

Let's take the example of feeling ill will toward someone who has stolen from us. When we become aware of the feeling of ill will and its associated thoughts, we can do an ABCD for a more helpful way to think. Wise, compassionate truths like, 'I'm not sure what is happening in their life to drive them to steal; I hope they get the support and help they need' can override our anger.

Feeling compassion instead of ill will doesn't mean we should just let people steal from us, but it does mean we wish for the person to receive the support they need so they don't steal again. By not wishing harm on another, it also ensures we're not creating causes for more harm to come to us in the future.

I understand this is a very high bar (world record high!) to reach, and it takes some practice to transform ill will into compassion, but it's in our own best interest to do so. My friend Hilary once reminded me that when it feels difficult to feel compassion for someone, it can help to just wish that I could.

As antidotes to ill will, compassion and empathy free us from taking perverse pleasure in the suffering of others. The karmic results of cultivating compassion and empathy are wonderful in that we experience trust, friendliness, and support from others.

Brené Brown offers us helpful advice in this area too. She tells us in her book *Daring Greatly*, 'Empathy is a strange and powerful thing. There is no script. There is no right way or wrong way to do it. It's simply listening, holding space, withholding judgement, emotionally connecting and communicating that incredibly healing message of, 'You're not alone'. [5] This quote offers us a way to practice empathy: all we need to do is listen without judgment and be there to connect and communicate that we are there with them.

Compassion involves the ability to be able to stand in another person's shoes and Pema Chödrön reminds us that compassionate action must start with ourselves. She says in her book *Start Where You Are*, 'If we are willing to stand fully in our own shoes and never give up on ourselves, then we will be able to put ourselves in the shoes of others and never give up on them.' [6]

This ability to put ourselves in others' shoes is essential for compassion. If we can understand what it is like for someone else, we're more able to replace judgment and ill-will with compassion. We also never know what is going on for another person or how they have arrived where they are, so it's far more helpful to be compassionate than judgmental.

Of course, this doesn't mean we shouldn't stick up for ourselves or others to prevent harm. But leading with compassion helps us tune in to our wise self, ensuring we don't perpetuate suffering.

Another way we can enjoy a good life relates to the viewpoints we hold. This guideline is up next.

Guideline Ten: Establish Accurate Viewpoints

The tenth guideline helps us navigate life with wisdom and compassion. It relates to avoiding erroneous views and embracing accurate ones.

Wow, we've reached the tenth (and final) misdeed to help us live happier lives. Let's briefly review the previous nine so we're ready for that next learning.

The first three relate to actions of the body:

1. **Don't kill**—protect and honour life
2. **Don't steal**—treat other people's things with respect and practice generosity
3. **Don't hurt others with your sexual activity**—respect and foster others' relationships

The next four relate to speech:

4. Don't lie—tell the truth
5. **Don't use your words to drive a wedge between people**—speak in ways that bring people together
6. **Don't hurt people with your words**—use words that are kind and pleasing to others
7. **Don't engage in useless speech**—make your words meaningful and sincere

The last three relate to the mind:

8. **Don't be envious of other people's lives**—rejoice in the little things that bring pleasure to others
9. **Don't be happy about other people's pain or problems**—be compassionate and empathetic

So let's now turn to our final guideline related to the mind:

10. Don't adhere to erroneous views—adopt viewpoints that are correct.

In the Buddhist tradition, this final misdeed—holding inaccurate worldviews—is considered the most damaging to our peace of mind. It makes us wrongly believe that misdeeds are permissible and without consequence.

The word 'erroneous', from the Latin root 'wrong' refers here to views such as: denying the laws of karma (thinking 'what goes around comes around' is untrue); believing there is no need for ethics or morality; adopting nihilistic views like 'nothing we really do matters' and 'life is meaningless'.

I summarise these incorrect views along the lines of: 'Nothing harmful, immoral, or illegal that I do or say will have any detrimental consequences to me as long as I don't get caught'. This is obviously a corrosive belief system, especially when lived out and expressed with certainty. It causes loads of negative karma and a world of problems.

The karmic consequences of holding these harmful views include: a tendency to be attracted to such beliefs in the future; finding ourselves surrounded by others who share these erroneous views; mistaking wrong for right, and believing that it's okay to harm others without consequence. It also includes finding it difficult to think clearly; and feeling we are stupid. That's a whole lot of not great consequences we want to avoid for ourselves and others!

Some texts indicate that the karmic consequences of this misdeed can include self-destructive tendencies and that holding steadfastly to such incorrect views leads us further into delusion and ignorance, both associated with more suffering and harm.

So, when we talk about adopting viewpoints that are correct, we are referring to embracing the worldview of karmic causality. This is the understanding of how things truly work, present in both the Eastern and Western wisdom traditions. I'm particularly drawn to the positive consequence that by practicing kind words and thoughts to ourselves and others, we are creating the causes for a world that's safe, kind, and welcoming. Here's to that!

HEART-FRIENDLY WAYS TO PRACTICE

Thank you for reviewing the last seven of the ten guidelines for living a good life! Let's close by putting a new habit into place.

You may like to:

- Choose one habit related to the guidelines that you would like to change—start small.
- Be mindful of the all-inclusive nature of lying and practice not giving anyone an impression that misrepresents what you believe to be true.
- Be inclusive with your speech. Introduce others into a group.
- Be on the lookout for harsh, hurtful speech, both external and your internal dialogue. Remember to check in with your wise self for speech that is kind and encouraging to everyone.
- Be aware of not joining in harmful gossip or speaking for the sake of speaking.
- Practice following through on commitments by doing what you say you will do.
- Practice piling onto the happiness of others. Choose to be happy for those who have good fortune.
- Be aware of the tendency to be happy about others' misfortune and instead bring compassion to mind.

Let's feel glad for all the positive energy we have created together and dedicate this to the happiness and wellbeing of all.

Join me in the next section when you are ready. It's all about how we can free ourselves by truly living in the present moment.

Lying can get us into strife

1. Maguire, Sharon, director. *'Bridget Jones's Baby'*, (Universal Pictures, 2016).

2. Aesop (n.d), *The Boy Who Cried Wolf.* (Aesop's Fables 1985).

Be your own best friend

3. Helen Reddy, *Best Friend*, Genius Site: https://genius.com/Helen-reddy-best-friend-lyrics

Follow your heart

4. J.A.D and Banks, C, *The Essential Rumi*, (San Francisco CA: Harper 1995).

Empathy—a strange and powerful thing

5. Brené Brown, *Daring Greatly: How Courage to be Vulnerable Transforms the Way We Live, Love, Parent and Lead*, (Gotham Books, 2012)

Compassion

6. Pema Chödrön, *Start Where You Are: A Guide to Compassionate Living* (Shambhala, 1994).

6. DEFRAZZLING

Coming Back to the Present

DEFRAZZLING

Learning to 'Be Here Now' helps us defrazzle; fostering calm, peace of mind, and contentment. What follows are easy and helpful ways and meditations to focus our minds on the now, instead of dwelling on the past or worrying about the future. It's freeing to realise the only time we truly have is the present moment, and when we bring ourselves back here, everything is all right.

Wherever You Are, Be There

Tap into present-moment awareness and learn effective strategies to cultivate mindfulness, enhance focus, and manage negative distractions.

While writing this book I sometimes lost concentration, either jumping ahead to fret about all the tasks still to do or going back in time and reliving feelings of being ill-equipped and unworthy to even try. It was only by bringing myself back to the present and tapping into the energy that was guiding me to finish, that I was able to tap, tap, tap the words out. I was so glad I had learned how to be in the moment, and the practices in this section are all about helping us find that state in our daily lives.

Why is it beneficial to cultivate present-moment awareness? Spiritual teacher Eckhart Tolle, in his book, *The Power of Now*[1] emphasises the importance of realising that the present moment is all we have. This serves as a reminder to stay present to avoid getting caught up elsewhere. An anonymous quote I like to remember is, 'Wherever you are, be there'.

For many, the mind incessantly dwells in the past or speculates on the future, often consumed by worries about what has already occurred or what may or may not happen. Both past regrets and future uncertainties exist only in the present mind, typically accompanied by anxiety. However, dwelling on the past or worrying about the future serves no useful purpose; it only serves to disturb our present state of mind.

So, how do we prevent past worries from spoiling our present? First let's look at the benefits of attempting it.

Training our minds to be present yields numerous benefits:

- By staying in the present moment, we avoid being distracted by past regrets or future worries.
- We experience a sense of calm and are less prone to the overwhelm of negative thoughts and emotions.
- Being present enables us to better connect with our surroundings and others.
- It enhances our ability to concentrate, exercise patience, and manage negative emotions.

Thankfully, there are strategies to train our minds to be more present and less preoccupied with past and future concerns. These practices are all coming up and are also available as audio meditations at mareeallanfolwer.com, and include:

- Embracing the 'Be Here Now' mindset as a grounding practice before meditation and at other times too.
- Practicing mindful breathing, using the breath as an anchor to the present moment.
- Reflecting on whether a memory serves a useful purpose in the present.
- Lama Marut's 'It's Like This Now' practice.

Are you ready to begin?

Preparing to Meditate So You Can 'Be Here Now'

Understanding the power of living in the present moment trains our minds to be free. Learning how to meditate can bring us there.

There are several benefits to training our minds to be in the present. However, it takes effort because, if you're like me, your mind may often be flitting hundreds of steps ahead or behind.

When I first learned about meditation and began a regular meditation practice some things that really helped me included:

- Having a **clean room or space** to go to each morning.
- Setting up a **small altar** with meaningful objects, photos or flowers in that space.
- Having a **comfortable cushion or chair** on which to sit and meditate
- Making a **regular time** to do my meditation practice.

While this works if I'm at home and in my regular routine, when I'm not, I need to make adjustments or be flexible and find alternatives. For example, when I travel with my husband, I might do a quick mindful run or walk, or do the preliminaries while he showers.

'Preliminaries' are just the small things we do at the beginning to help ourselves settle before we meditate. I often start our POM yoga practice with the following.

Meditation Preliminaries:

- Sit in a comfortable meditation position, whatever feels right for you. Close your eyes. Check your posture.
- Feel the bottom of your body supported by the cushion, block, chair or floor.
- Let go of any tension in the legs.
- Feel a long, straight back by lifting the heart and relaxing the shoulders.
- Let the arms rest comfortably in the lap or on the knees.
- Feel the head evenly balanced on the shoulders.
- Let go of any tension in the shoulders, across the chest, and in the neck.
- Relax the jaw, mouth, and smooth out the face and scalp.
- Let the eyes rest comfortably in their sockets.
- Feel a pole of energy running through the body and relax the body around it.
- Do a final scan for any tension in the body and release it.

Now take three breaths—inhale deeply through the nostrils and exhale gently through the mouth, with an audible sigh.

Repeat this process three times. This assists with settling the sympathetic (which is not so sympathetic to relaxing) nervous system.

Sometimes I add the 'Be Here Now' meditation to my preliminaries to bring myself into the present before moving onto a more specific contemplation. This is a very versatile exercise and doesn't need to be restricted to formal meditation practice.

Lama Marut refers to this practice as 'setting our internal GPS'. We can use it anytime we like and it simply involves orienting ourselves in time and place, where and when we are.

The 'Be Here Now' meditation:

We bring our attention to our surroundings, leaving behind where we've come from and where we're headed next, becoming aware of our current location, the room we're in, and the people we're with.

We then become aware of where we are in the ever-changing present moment. We do this by tuning into the changing nature of the present using our senses:

- **First**, we attend to any sounds we can hear—notice the many changing sounds around us.
- **Next**, we notice the sensations we can feel—notice the pressure or warmth on the skin, without needing to analyse.
- **Finally**, we bring our attention to any lingering smells—notice the scents of nature or fragrance of a home.

After this meditation preliminary practice, we bring our attention to the breath, with a simple mindful breathing meditation, which is coming up next.

The Mindful Breath Meditation

This simple breath observation helps cultivate present-moment awareness and enhanced focus.

Mindfulness is the ability to pay careful attention to our thoughts, feelings, and sensations in the present moment without judging them as good or bad. Mindfulness can assist us in managing difficult emotions such as anger and sadness or emotional responses such as stress or anxiety.

One method for cultivating mindfulness is to focus our attention on our breath. By dedicating time to practice mindful breathing, we train ourselves to redirect our focus to the breath in our daily lives. This enhances our ability to concentrate, exercise patience and cope with negative emotions.

This breath meditation—or even remembering to tune into the breath during our daily lives—offers numerous benefits including:

- Enhancing our ability to focus on the breath, thus bringing us into the present moment.
- Facilitating concentration, patience and the management of negative emotions.
- Anchoring us in the present moment—preventing distraction by past regrets and future worries.
- Providing us with an anchor that promotes calmness and prevents us from being swept away by unhelpful thoughts and emotions.

To practice the 'Mindful Breath Meditation', first do the preliminary practices as outlined in the previous reflection: settle into a comfortable meditation posture, perform three inhales through the nostrils followed by sigh exhales through the mouth, and then engage in the 'Be Here Now' meditation.

We then shift our attention to the breath which serves as our anchor in the present moment. Since we are always breathing in the present moment, directing our attention here helps settle the mind into the present.

Concentrate the mind on the breath, observing the inhale passing through the nostrils, the brief pause, and the exhale exiting through the nostrils. We needn't manipulate the breath; simply observe it.

While doing this, our minds may wander to other things, which is perfectly normal. It's beneficial to recognise when our minds wander. When this occurs, gently guide the mind back to the breath, akin to guiding a wandering toddler. Relax and repeat this process as often as necessary.

Remain focused on the breath for five minutes, redirecting attention when required. Remember to be gentle and encouraging with your wandering mind. We all require gentle guidance, particularly when new to meditation.

If you find it helpful to provide the mind with a focus during this mindful breath meditation, you can practice a 'cycle of ten breaths'. This entails noting each exhale and mentally counting one, then two on the next exhale, and so forth up to ten. If the mind becomes distracted and loses count, simply return to counting from one again, kindly.

We can tune into the breath at any moment by directing our attention to it, wherever we are. This grounds us in the present, where everything is usually alright or if not, it is at least 'like this now'.

To learn more about the useful concept of 'it's like this now', join me in the next chapter.

It's Like This Now

The 'It's Like This Now' practice is worth a try as it guides us to an acceptance of the present moment and fosters wiser, more compassionate responses to life's challenges.

The 'It's Like This Now' practice or tool is incredibly helpful for bringing us into the present, preventing us from what Byron Katie refers to as 'arguing with reality'. She says, 'I am a lover of what is. Why? Because it hurts when I argue with reality.' [2]

Accepting how things are now and questioning what my wisest response might be to what is unfolding, allows me to avoid blame, conflict, and criticism—and instead respond with more wisdom. Practicing this has saved me a lot of worry over many years.

By realising that 'it's like this now', we bring ourselves back into the present—the now—and as the present moment is constantly changing, we have to keep up!

Almost always, everything is perfectly okay in the present too, unless we're in a fast unfolding situation in which we are at physical risk. In most situations in the present though, there's no fear or worry needed and they only arise when we place our minds in the past or the future, which is the ultimate waste of time.

This practice helps us accept and embrace the present. When something unwanted happens or when we don't get what we want, we may have a tendency to wish it were different. My mind, for example, can protest with cries of 'You should not have said that hurtful thing to me', 'It shouldn't be raining', or 'They should have called me', when clearly, they *have* said that hurtful thing, it *is* raining, and they *haven't* called!

No amount of protesting, complaining, or wishing it were different is going to help. All I am doing is ruining my present and future peace of mind. So, what might be a more helpful response?

I'm not saying this is easy and that's because it requires radical acceptance of what is happening instead of arguing with reality. Acceptance is not apathy either. It's about the courage and willingness to acknowledge things are 'like this now'. It's about turning problems into opportunities, such as viewing 'badly' timed rain as benefiting the garden.

I really do find 'it's like this now' to be an incredibly useful thing to say to myself, and I follow it with the ABCD practice. Why? Because when I can Accept that the situation is *like this now*, instead of how I think it should or shouldn't have been, I bring myself into the present where it's much easier to Breathe. Then I can Connect with my wiser self which brings with it love, compassion and wisdom, and I follow up by asking, 'Given that it's like this now, what's the wisest thing to Do?'

And as you might guess, the best response is not to be a victim with blame, criticism, or protest, but rather to Accept and tune into wisdom—to let go of the hurtful thing someone said, or to embrace the volatile weather, or bring understanding and forgiveness to my friend for not calling. It may also help me gather the courage to have a difficult conversation with a friend who broke a promise. Can you see how this practice can allow us to turn a so-called problem into an opportunity?

A similar helpful phrase we might say to ourselves in situations like this is: 'It is what it is', although I do prefer 'It's like this now. There's also a version for when things get much, much worse, it's: 'Even This'.

Even when we're dealing with an 'even this' situation, it's liberating to realise that if there is something to be done, we can do it and not worry; and if there is nothing we can do, we can do nothing and not worry.

Practicing acceptance allows me to do as yoga teacher Andrew Mournehis suggests and 'Be Bamboo', which is strong yet flexible. I've been trying to remember to 'be bamboo' as I write and rewrite during the Chinese New Year of the Wood Dragon!

And what about when memories intrude into our current thoughts? Let's discuss that next.

Is This Memory Useful for Me Now?

Learn to ask yourself —'Is this memory useful for me now? By doing so, you teach yourself to let go of past and future worries.

Another method that helps train our mind to be more present is to ask ourselves the question, 'Is this memory useful for me now?'

This is a simple question we can ask whenever a memory from the past intrudes upon our present moment, disrupting our peace of mind. We can inquire whether this memory contributes to our current state of tranquility, and if not, we can let it go, and take a few breaths to return to the present.

For instance, when happily engaging with a friend, the memory of a past time they made a mean comment about my outfit might pop into my mind. This memory is clearly not useful for our present, peaceful interaction. Another example is when attempting an activity like pottery, and the memory of a previous mishap surfaces, undermining our confidence to proceed. Is this memory useful for me now? Clearly not.

A second question that may prove useful to ask is: 'Is worrying about the future, about what may or may not happen, useful for me now?' The answer is always no, because worry is invariably a squandering of our precious time. It sabotages the only time we possess—the present. Who knows what the future holds?

A saying I find helpful to remind myself of this is, ‘Embrace the present, let go of the past, and trust the future’. As Lama Marut says, if something undesirable occurs and we can take action, then let’s do so and refrain from worrying; if we cannot do anything about it, then let’s do nothing and refrain from worrying.

None of this precludes us from planning for the future or remembering the past. But, from a mindful, present and peaceful state of mind, when we revisit these times that have already passed or are yet to come, we can do so with wisdom instead of worry.

Another strategy I find helpful in alleviating future worries is to tell myself, ‘I am not going to worry about that now. I will allocate some time, say at 6 p.m. tonight, to worry about it.’ Usually, by the time the designated worry time arrives, I’ve forgotten what was causing me concern anyway!

Sometimes though, when leeches have literally attached to you, it can be difficult to put the worry off. Let’s chat about that next.

Lost! Leeches! Oh, It's Like this Now.

The liberating practice of 'It's Like This Now—What Is My Wisest Response?' transforms angst into acceptance, fostering growth amidst challenges.

The 'It's Like This Now—What Is My Wisest Response?' tool is so helpful. In many situations it has saved me from angst and unhelpful reactions to what is happening in the now. As Byron Katie says, 'Got stress? You are arguing with reality.' [3]

So how do I argue with reality? For me, it's my non-acceptance of how things are and the inner protest that somehow, they should be different from how they actually are. And as Byron Katie says, it is stressful to do so!

When I'm able to accept *it's like this now*, tune in for a wise response, and follow through, I can choose to let go of needing a certain result. I can trust all is unfolding as it's meant to. It's so freeing! It allows me to find the blessing or life lesson and turn the so-called problem into an opportunity to change my patterns of reactive behaviour; cultivate empathy in situations where I'd normally be judgmental; or take compassionate action to change something harmful.

I was reminded of this several times during a trip to Sri Lanka, where, instead of arguing with reality, I had the opportunity to practice acceptance of many so-called unwanted situations. I tried to remember to apply a wise response—although not always on the spot as the following examples outline!

One such experience was on a walk in the beautiful hill country near Ella, where my friend Kate and I got lost, fell into a stream, and were set upon by leeches. My protests included: 'the map should be better', 'they should have told us about the leeches', 'this shouldn't be happening' and 'this is going to be a disaster'. I was swearing, slightly hysterical and completely frazzled.

This certainly didn't help the situation. The protests of blame, non-acceptance and fear were certainly not my wisest response to what was happening in the moment, being geographically lost but well and truly found by legions of leeches.

Fortunately, Kate kept it together for both of us, finding a reference point that helped us head in the right direction. So, what was the blessing for me in this situation? To accept, check in with my wise self for what to do instead of arguing with reality, and to trust. (And later, to let myself off the hook for freaking out during what was, in fairness, quite a scary situation!)

All ended well: we met some lovely people who helped us and we all had such a good laugh about our adventure. We discovered that leeches are harmless in the long term, we had fun turning our room into a temporary first aid centre, and we now have a great, if squeamish story to share.

Have you ever discovered an unexpected blessing after experiencing difficulty? There's a deeper practice of 'It's Like This Now' which you might like to contemplate in the next chapter.

It's Like This Now: Excess Baggage

Deepen your practice of 'It's Like This Now—What Is My Wisest Response?' by embracing acceptance, preventing conflict and discovering unexpected blessings in difficulties.

As previously outlined, this tool is so helpful for bringing us into the present and preventing us from arguing with reality. Acceptance of how it is now and questioning our wisest response to what is unfolding, allows us to prevent blame, conflict and criticism, and to respond appropriately.

Sri Lanka provided me with another reminder of the invaluable benefits of 'It's Like This Now—What Is My Wisest Response?' when I had the opportunity to accept the reality of arriving at the airport with excess baggage. I was bringing home handwoven fabric and goods I had purchased for POM to sell here in support of our projects. I can recall my mind going into blame, victim, and criticism mode as it argued with the reality of having too much luggage. I was blaming myself and the airline with protests of 'This is not fair; I should not be in this situation' and 'Why do they have luggage restrictions anyway?!'

Fortunately, I remembered to question whether this was useful and concluded it wasn't. What did I need to do? Accept it's like this now and tune into my wise self for a helpful response—and try to trust that all would unfold as it was meant to.

Again, that truism I find so useful is relevant: Embrace the present, let go of the past, and trust the future.

I came up with the idea to decide to see the extortionate excess baggage fee like the money I could have spent on a business class upgrade. So, I paid the money and told myself now I was traveling business class.

As it transpired, the plane was fairly full, and I found myself seated next to a woman whose partner was seated next to a non-related toddler a few rows ahead of us. I offered to swap seats with her partner so they could be together—although I do remember thinking a long flight next to a toddler may be a bit tricky! 'Thanks, but no need. I think my partner has it sorted' was her reply. I settled in, feeling peaceful, when shortly after take-off she disappeared to join her partner in another row altogether, leaving me with two seats to myself—thank you for my business upgrade!

So, yet again, when you can Accept with 'It's Like This Now', check in to your wise self for what to Do, and let go and trust, it is a lot easier to work with reality. By embracing this idea, the same situation I had initially responded to with criticism, anger and worry, had been transformed into quite a fun, comfortable trip home. It gave my reality a business class upgrade too!

The practice coming up in the next chapter can also transport you, and in just five minutes!

The Five Minute Shavasana

This 'Five Minute Shavasana' practice, derived from yoga, is designed for daily use to enhance tranquility and mental clarity.

Shavasana, a common yoga practice for relaxation and restoration for mind and body, is typically done at the end of a yoga session, but can be done at any time. I warmly invite you to start and maintain this simple, effective practice, as taking time to relax and restore is essential for well-being and makes us more present for others too.

Here's a condensed five-minute version, recommended by yoga teacher Andrew Mournehis for daily practice. He recommends doing it each and every day—for the rest of our lives.

1. **Find a comfortable spot to lie down.**
   If lying down isn't possible, a comfy chair can be a suitable alternative

2. **Place an eye pillow over your eyes, or simply close them.**
   This helps us focus and go within.

3. **Relax your body.**
   If lying down, extend your arms out from your body with your palms facing up. Using a quick progressive relaxation scan, bring your attention to and relax your feet, legs, pelvic area, torso, chest, arms and hands, neck, jaw, mouth, face and scalp.

A relaxed body is good for our well-being. We are often unaware of the tension we hold in our body, particularly in the jaw, neck and shoulders.

By becoming aware of our body holding stress or tightness, we can simply think 'relax the body' and allow ourselves to release it. When I teach yoga, I am constantly reminding myself and others to check in with the wisdom of the body—which prompts us to relax and let go of tension

4. **Release any thoughts that arise.**
   Consider thoughts like passing clouds, observing them with joyful indifference as they come and go, leaving our peace undisturbed.

5. **Return to the breath.**
   Gently redirect your attention to the breath whenever the mind wanders. Observe the sensations of breathing at the nostrils or the chest, and if distracted, kindly return to the breath without self-criticism.

6. **Repeat steps three to five.**
   Continue this loop for five minutes. When the time has been reached, perhaps wiggle your fingers or toes, then, gently open your eyes. If lying down, roll to one side, and slowly rise.

Some Helpful Tips:

You may like to set a timer—a kitchen timer works well—so you're not concerned about the time. It's best to avoid using your phone, as it can be distracting; perhaps even place it in another room.

When your mind strays from the breath (which if you're anything like me, it will!) be a kind, encouraging friend who gently guides it back. I've found I'm more receptive to a kind approach than a harsh, critical, taskmaster one. Replacing the unhelpful, inner voice with a kind one is always beneficial and practicing positive self-talk in meditation helps create this habit.

If finding five minutes or a suitable quiet spot during a busy workday is challenging, consider practicing after work or in the evening. Alternatively, you can sit or lie down in a park during lunchtime.

I encourage you to give this Shavasana practice a try. You have nothing to lose at all—except perhaps some stress! Others will appreciate a more relaxed you, too.

HEART-FRIENDLY WAYS TO PRACTICE

Thank you for reading these reflections and reaching the end of this section on defrazzling!

Please join me in rejoicing in the fact that we and others have read, contemplated or practiced these meditations and reflections.

Maybe you would like to give some of them a try now!

Let's feel glad for all the positive energy we have created together and dedicate this to the happiness and wellbeing of all.

Pile on!

And pile into the next section which is all about growing our compassion and peace of mind.

Live in the present

1. Eckhart Tolle, *The Power of Now*, (Hodder Paperback, 2001).

Stop Arguing with reality

2. Byron Katie, *How to Stop Arguing with Reality*, (Harper Collins, 2001).

3. Ibid.

7. FOSTERING COMPASSION & PEACE OF MIND

FOSTERING COMPASSION & PEACE OF MIND

Showing compassion toward ourselves and others is always good for our peace of mind and contentment. Exploring practices to grow compassion, including 'Thank You for Reminding Me' and 'Just Like Me', helps put ourselves in another's shoes, allowing for empathy and compassion. We'll also look at overcoming the pitfalls of pride and low self-confidence through a better *for* other's attitude shift.

Thank You for Reminding Me

Appreciate what is truly going on and where our emotions are coming from by remembering to be aware, followed by doing our ABCD: Acceptance, Breath, Connect, Doing

The 'Thank You For Reminding Me' practice helps reduce the tendency to be judgmental and increases the ability to be compassionate.

It begins with the ABCD practice, starting with *awareness* of the emotion being triggered. Maybe you have been hooked by someone's words or actions, and then anger, irritation, jealously, hurt, or sadness has bubbled up. Accept what is going on, and resist the temptation to suppress, feed, or inappropriately express. Take a Breath to Connect to your wise, intuitive self for what to Do, then act appropriately.

Sometimes, when I'm triggered, this process leads me to ask myself, 'What is this person or event reminding me?' Particularly with the Doing step, I say to myself: *Thank you for reminding me to be kind* if I am perceiving unkindness; *Thank you for reminding me to be attentive* if I am perceiving distraction; *Thank you for reminding me to be patient* if I am perceiving impatience.

Additionally, it's very helpful to separate the behaviour from the person. When we perceive someone's behaviour is impatient or rude, rather than thinking or saying *they are rude*, consider instead that *they are behaving rudely*. This is a subtle but important distinction to help reduce judgment and foster more compassion, empathy and connection.

This simple question, 'What is this person (who is behaving rudely) reminding me?', reveals that it's not nice for anyone when they behave unkindly—including themselves. Holding compassion for them, and for yourself, naturally arises, and you may even genuinely thank them for the reminder to be kind and patient. It may not be appropriate to express this thanks verbally—thinking it may be less inflammatory.

This approach can easily slip into sounding self-righteous or insincere if we're coming from a place of feeling superior. But when we respond with genuine sincerity—by taking responsibility for our part in the moment, and by recognising that we ourselves have acted this way in the past—compassion and connection arise far more naturally.

Taking accountability for similar behaviour from our own history isn't an invitation to criticise ourselves or to feel ashamed either Instead, it's a gentle reminder to be grateful for yet another opportunity to learn

This isn't all about focussing on negativity either, we can also say 'Thank You For Reminding Me' when positive emotions are triggered. When someone gives us a smile and it feels good, we can thank the person for their kind reminder—whether out loud or in thought, whatever is appropriate.

It's so easy for our funny minds to be cynical and sarcastic, finding the negative in situations. So, whenever we're reminded to be kind, joyful, grateful, or generous, we can genuinely give thanks to whomever and whatever helps bring us back to those wonderful feelings.

The practice and question—*What is this person or event reminding me?* — is helpful when we feel triggered and want to respond in a more compassionate, less judgmental manner to both ourselves and others. As I've discovered though, it can be difficult to do when strong emotions are involved!

Once I remember becoming angry over a manager's accommodation booking bungle and subsequent refund refusal. There was an inappropriate expression of anger on my part. I perceived the manager's behaviour to be dishonest and manipulative, and told him so with an angry outburst, 'You are behaving like a f****** asshole!' Whoops! Clearly, I dedicated no time to ABCD in the heat of the moment!

I'm not saying I shouldn't have outlined and detailed my case in the booking discrepancy—I don't regret negotiating the injustice perceived. I do, however, regret the heated outburst that may have caused harm.

Tempted as I was to give myself a very hard time over my extreme reaction, when things calmed down I instead took a Breath and Connected to my wise self. By doing so, I was able to experience clearer thoughts and understanding. I realised I could release the energy of anger I was experiencing physically through a brisk walk, run, or some yoga. I could also ring a trusted friend—someone who would understand, show empathy, and not be judgmental. Someone who could simply listen to what had happened without feeling the need to placate, offer unsolicited advice, sympathy, shame, blame, or express disapproval or disappointment in me. Fortunately, friends like this exist, and I am grateful for their empathy and understanding.

It's human to make mistakes and not always be in tune with wisdom, and it's also human to forget to use the tools shared with us.

Forgiveness and self-compassion are healing.

And so what did this person or event remind me? The experience taught me about checking booking details carefully and how to negotiate more skillfully and kindly.

But I also received an opportunity to practice something deeper: self-compassion and forgiveness. We can always be grateful for reminders that bring us back to this.

And sometimes we need some extra reminders, which the practice in the next chapter gives us.

'Just Like Me' Compassion Practice

Pema Chödrön's 'Just Like Me' practice fosters compassion and understanding. In this reflection, we'll explore it further.

Compassion is one of the core Buddhist practices that helps us to step out of our ego-created armour and into another person's shoes. It softens the heart and allows us to feel what another might be experiencing. Doing this calls for not only open-heartedness, but for courage too.

Pema Chödrön outlines a very helpful practice entitled 'Just Like Me' in her book *Welcoming the Unwelcome: Wholehearted Living in a Broken World.* [1] This mindset allows us to develop compassion and reduce judgment and criticism.

When we find ourselves in an unwelcome situation—like being stuck in a traffic jam, waiting in a slow-moving queue, or feeling alone or scared—instead of looking around to see the problems or apparent causes of the situation, we can look around and zero in on someone in this same situation and say to ourselves, 'Just like me, this person has somewhere to go, and they are feeling frustrated by being held up.'

We can also do this practice when we see someone, for example, lose their temper, look uncomfortable, work hard at pleasing others (or trying to be liked), or acting in a difficult or argumentative way. By simply saying to ourselves, 'Just like me, this person is feeling angry, feels uncomfortable, wants to be liked, or is feeling defiant,' we are fostering compassion, understanding, and connection.

We can never really know what these strangers are thinking or feeling, but doing this practice can help us remember we are all similar and in the same boat. By doing so, our interactions with others become more empathetic and expansive.

It is important that we do not use this 'Just Like Me' practice as another way to focus on our unhelpful habits and beat ourselves up. For example, if we see someone losing it in traffic, rather than dispassionately judging them or ourselves, we can instead see this as an opportunity for a shared compassionate understanding. We are all human; we can all lose it. And we can all use a situation like this as an opportunity to drop judgment and be kind, encouraging, and compassionate towards ourselves and others.

The 'Just Like Me' practice can be used when we see great things happening too! For example, if we observe someone helping another, we can think, 'just like me, this person is being kind.' This gives us an opportunity to rejoice in their kindness and ours too, which makes us all feel good, reinforcing the positive things we are doing in the world.

Sometimes though, we can do with some extra tools for managing difficult people, and that's what you'll discover in the next chapter.

Disappearing the Irritating Person in Three Steps

Learn to manage irritation gracefully with a three-step strategy cultivating more patience and compassion in challenging interactions.

Many years ago, Lama Marut taught me a cheekily named strategy for dealing with challenging people: *Disappearing the Irritating Person in Three Steps*. Despite the title, no one is harmed, banished, or magically erased. What *does* disappear, over time, is our reactivity.

This approach has helped me cultivate more patience and compassion, and it's also shown me that responding with irritation only keeps the cycle going—while suppressing it doesn't help either.

When I first heard the name of the strategy, I couldn't help but smile. If only we could click our fingers to remove our troubles. I'm fairly sure that, like me, you have at least one person in your life who knows exactly how to press your buttons. Since disappearing them isn't an option, learning how to work with irritation—without tipping into anger, criticism, or silent seething—becomes an essential life skill.

The strategy involves three steps that build upon each other as our patience grows. First, it's essential to *accept* and acknowledge the feeling of irritation without suppressing or expressing it.

Then, we can follow these steps:

1. **Get out of there:**

   Rather than react with anger or criticism, Lama Marut's advice in these moments is simple: remove yourself from the situation to avoid escalating conflict. That is, when you feel the irritation arise, 'get out of there'—perhaps by saying you need to use the bathroom. You don't have to say why you're leaving, but you may be able to think of other creative ways to exit a situation with respect and truth.

2. **Bump on a Log' or Breathe:**

   When we've had a bit of practice with Step 1, we're ready for a Buddhist practice called 'Bump on a Log', which simply means: don't react—stay like a bump on a log. That is, when we feel irritation, we don't respond with irritation.

   I misunderstood this practice for many years, using it as a way to suppress the irritation I was feeling, which of course, is not helpful.

   To counteract my tendency to suppress or bypass emotions when irritation arises, I now try not to react on autopilot. Instead, I notice it, acknowledge it and breathe through it.

   We often suppress irritation because it feels uncomfortable and we just want it gone. But we can instead accept the feeling and even get curious about where it's showing up in the body. Then simply breathe.

   If we can stick with the discomfort, and breathe

mindfully, the feeling will lighten, and we will be freer to *respond* from a more helpful spot, rather than *react* out of habit.

3. **Feel compassion:**

   This step requires work and builds on the first two, it's about understanding that angry or difficult people are often suffering themselves. When we can feel compassion instead of irritation, we effectively 'disappear' the irritating person because we're now responding from a place of understanding rather than reacting from habit.

Zen master Thich Nhat Hanh explains that when someone makes you suffer—by causing irritation, getting angry at you or hurting you—it's because they're suffering deeply themselves, and their pain is spilling over. He suggests that this person doesn't need punishment or for us to retaliate back with anger or hurt. What they really need is help and compassion. That is the message they are sending, even if they don't know it. Another helpful way to put it is: *hurt people hurt people.*

A friend, Hilary, gave me some great advice when I was struggling to feel compassion. She suggested I acknowledge my feelings and express the desire to feel differently by saying to myself, 'I don't feel compassion right now, but I wish I did'. This acknowledges the truth of how I feel along with my aspiration to change, which sows seeds for compassion to arise in the future.

I'm grateful for Hilary's advice, because Step 3 of disappearing an irritating person can sometimes feel harder than pulling a rabbit out of a hat!

But what if we're the irritating one? Find out about a fun complaining-fast to try next.

A 24-Hour Complaining-Fast

Try a 24-hour 'complaining fast'.
Observe your inner dialogue and discover
the power of wise responses.

I once boldly declared I would attempt to go 24 hours without complaining (at least outwardly!) to others.

Interestingly, I woke on my 'complaining fast' day with a sore back. 'Oh no,' I thought, 'I said I wouldn't complain today, and now I have a sore back!' Now, I don't want you to misunderstand me here. Not complaining doesn't mean ignoring or suppressing pain and becoming a martyr. My back did hurt, so I acknowledged it, but decided to proceed with care and consideration for my tender back.

I observed my mind searching for a possible cause to blame for the pain and someone to criticise (including myself). Maybe it was the way I lifted something, the Pilates instructor's positioning, or the cold weather snap. But I was aware it was not useful to board that 'blame and complain' train.

So instead, I remembered my commitment to the 24-hour 'complaining fast', tuning into my wise self for advice. *Accepting* my sore back and moving through the day kindly, doing what I needed to do with care, seemed a wise way to go. When asked how I was, I simply said my back was reminding me to take things slowly today.

Throughout the day the complaining soundtrack in my head played on, and I was often tempted to give it a voice, but every time a thought of worry or complaint came up, I reassured my mind that I was being careful and was safe. I could do all I needed to do, just a little slower than usual. I was also buoyed by and grateful for the help of friends.

By checking in with my wise self and accepting the situation with kindness and compassion, I resisted the urge to:

- Suppress or push away the feeling or pain
- Ignore it by soldiering on with martyrdom
- Blame or criticise myself or others
- Feel sorry for myself and become a victim

Instead, I compassionately proceeded with care and consideration, breaking past unhelpful habits and getting on with what I needed to do—including taking some breaks.

It showed me that when something unwanted happens, instead of slipping into irritation— or becoming irritating ourselves through complaining, blaming, comparing or finding ourselves lacking—we can shift gears. Counting our blessings and recalling what we're grateful for can change the whole experience.

And, when we don't quite get it right, the appropriate response to any irritating person— including ourselves—is compassion.

My complaining-fast experiment resulted in a more compassionate day and plenty of opportunities to feel grateful. No complaints here!

And hopefully you'll have no complaints about the next chapter, which introduces a useful concept for times when we're lacking in confidence.

An Antidote to Low Self-Confidence

Understanding the pitfalls of pride and low self-confidence, embracing humility and cultivating the 'Better for Others' mindset-shift provides genuine self-improvement.

Pride and low self-confidence are, to me, two sides of the same coin, both stemming from comparing ourselves to others: are they better or worse than me? Superior or inferior? These thinking-styles do not reflect the whole truth, thus eroding our happiness and self-assurance.

Each of us is unique; with our own particular abilities, traits, and qualities. We're all better or worse than others at certain things—most people I know, for instance, are far, far better singers than me!—but those differences don't make us *essentially* better or worse than anyone else.

Low self-confidence or feelings of inferiority are very different to genuine humility. Humility does not mean downplaying your accomplishments or abilities. It means accepting that you are human and, as such, you have things you are talented at; but also make mistakes and have shortcomings. It also means being open to learning and growing from these experiences.

A humble person knows how to graciously accept a compliment, but does not seek them. They are able to admit their mistakes and ask for help when it is needed. Humility also shows that you value the opinions of others and do not consider yourself above them. Humble people let their actions and achievements speak for themselves.

The 'Better for Others' practice, which I learned from Lama Marut, helps me from slipping into self-doubt, feeling inferior, or 'worse than' others. It also helps me from slipping into feeling prideful or 'Better *Than* Others'.

The practice involves an intentional shift in mindset: to take the focus off of yourself and turn your attention to others. This shift reduces the stress associated with pride and lifts us out of self-doubt.

Simply put, we can think of it as doing our best to be better *for* others rather than better *than* others. When we have the intention of being better *for* others, it naturally uplifts us, and others too.

I can apply this mindset shift to anything I do: looking after my health, taking care of my appearance, giving a speech, or writing these reflections. By approaching these things with the intention of being better *for* others—and asking myself 'how can I be better for others?' —I find I move beyond my pride and low self-confidence and feel more joy and contentment.

Next, I will share an example of using this practice in my writing.

How 'Others' Helped Me Get Out of My Own Way

Shifting to a 'Better for Others' mindset in writing my blog dispels self-doubt, encourages genuine sharing, and aligns intentions with altruism.

Here is an example of using the 'Better for Others' practice in relation to my blog writing. I hope it will reveal how you might be able to apply it to a challenge in your own life.

When writing blogs and reflections I often experience a confidence wobble, doubting and questioning my ability. This voice criticises me, sets unrealistic expectations, compares me to others poorly, and expresses disbelief in my ability to share anything worthwhile. This focus on my shortcomings makes me feel worse. It's not a pleasant, peaceful, or happy state of mind to be in.

When I become *aware* of this negative self-talk, I turn to my everyday lifesaver, the ABCD:

- Accepting what's going on by saying 'thank you for sharing' to myself so that critical part of me feels heard
- taking a Breath and
- tuning into and Connecting with my wise self for what to Do.

It reminds me that these thoughts are not true and that a 'Better for Others' mindset shift is needed.

I remind myself that I am doing my best to write to be better *for* others, not to be better *than* others.

When I'm writing with the intention of being better *than* others, I find myself attempting to be the best writer around, or to receive accolades or approval from others about my writing. It is a stressful 'all about me' mindset. Conversely, when I have the worse-than-others critical inner voice, I am filled with doubt and low self-confidence—another stressful 'all about me' place.

When I ask myself, 'What is best *for* others?' and 'How can I be better *for* others?' I'm reminded to do my best to write to share things I've found useful. With this better-for-others intention, I find the pride and low self-confidence drops away, allowing me to share what has helped me. It also aids me in letting go of the result of whether others even read or find my writing useful.

Of course, I hope they do! However, I understand that whether they find it helpful is not up to me; the only control I have is over my intention to be of benefit.

This idea of letting go of the results of our actions is outlined in the Bhagavad Gita's [2] verses on *karma yoga*, the yoga of action. This is action done without worry about the outcome, such as whether the writing is helpful and received well. When we are able to do our best and then let go of attachment to the outcome, we become more relaxed and as a result, do a better job too.

We also become more relaxed when we allow ourselves time for self-care, and we cover that in the next chapter.

A Self-Care Tune-Up

We can give ourselves a self-care tune-up
with a 'Better for Others' mindset.
With the focus on others, we can feel good
and appreciate the benefits too.

An anonymous quote I love is *look good, feel good, do good.* It reminds me of the importance of taking care of my appearance and doing good. Not in a self-obsessed or vain way, but in the intention to help myself and others feel happy.

At times I can have a somewhat slack attitude towards taking extra time to look good, even when I know I could be making more effort. And at other times, I get competitive and put pressure on myself to look 'better *than* others'. Both of these attitudes are unhelpful.

A more beneficial attitude is to take care of my appearance, not just for my own sense of wellbeing, but because it can uplift others too. I know my mum always appreciated my making an effort, and I felt glad about making her happy too, taking extra care to dress nicely on hospital visits.

Our attempts to look good, do good or be better in any way can be driven by our intention to be of benefit *to* others rather than being better *than* others in a competitive way. When we make this shift to be 'better for others', there is no room for unhelpful pride or the equally unhelpful other side of the pride-coin.

Sarah Turnbull, in her memoir *Almost French,* [3] gives a great illustration of this 'better for others' intention. Living in Paris with her French partner, Frédéric, Sarah describes going to the bakery in her tracksuit pants and returning home to an appalled Frédéric. In response to her attire, he commented: 'It's not nice for the baker.' This reminds me that it feels good to make an effort to look after my appearance—not just for myself but for others too.

So, with this mindset-shift, I'm embracing a 'better for others' rebalance with some lipstick, mascara and hair care—and it feels good! The lipstick is a little challenging, as I am blessed with my Nan's thin lips and can easily miss them as Nan used to do!

Make-up may not be your thing, but some other activities might give you that tune-up feeling: haircare, a beard trim or shave, some new clothes or shoe clean, or even a nice 'beauty nap' may be your way of sprucing up—for those around you, and also for your own self-care service.

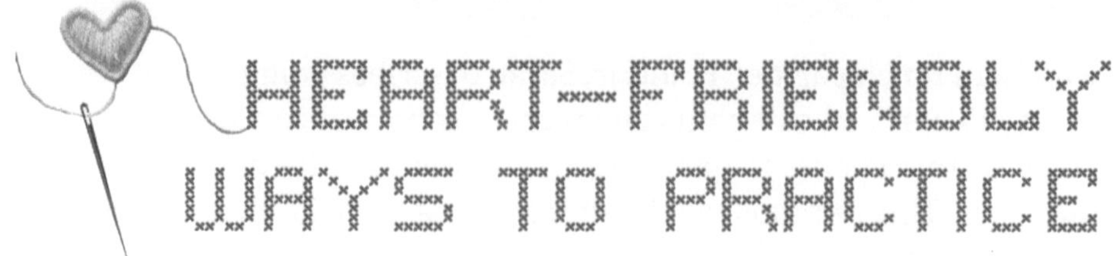

HEART-FRIENDLY WAYS TO PRACTICE

Given that this is the final reflection in this Section, please join me in rejoicing in the fact that we and others have read, contemplated or practiced these practices and reflections to foster our compassion and peace of mind.

xxxxxxxxxxxxxxxxxxxxxxxxxxxxxxxxxxxxxxxxxxxxxxxxxx

Maybe you would like to

- Be aware of feeling judgmental or frustrated about a behaviour you find annoying, for example, experiencing someone who impatiently pushes into a queue. Doing an ABCD to be reminded to think 'thank you for reminding me to be patient' instead of becoming impatient or judgemental in response will promote compassion for all.

- Practice 'just like me' as a way to develop compassion for someone who might be behaving in an unhelpful way. Remember thought to be kind to yourself and not to give yourself a hard time about when you have behaved similarly.

- Practice 'just like me' when you see someone behaving in a helpful way. This gives us an opportunity to feel happy about others and our own kindness.

- Give the 'disappearing the irritating person' practice a go! Practice with steps one and two to be able to get to step three and show compassion.

- Have a go at feeling happy for those who are happy. Pile on! Start with small things to be happy about and see how it feels, compared to feeling unhappy about their happiness.

- Try adopting a better for others in relation to something simple like having the confidence to learn a fresh skill like cooking something new.

- Give a 24-hour complaining fast a try. Maybe trying for a couple of hours would be a good place to start and then you can build up to longer stints.

Let's feel glad for all the positive energy we have created together and dedicate this to the happiness and wellbeing of all.

And we're going to create lots more positive energy in the next section by learning how to forgive.

SOURCES: **SECTION 7. FOSTERING COMPASSION & PEACE OF MIND**

Just like me

1. Pema Chödrön, *Welcoming the Unwelcome: Wholehearted Living in a Broken World*, (Shabahla, 2002.)

The Yoga of Action

2. Stephen Mitchell, *The Bhagavad Gita*, (NY Crown Publications, 2022).

Better for others

3. Sarah Turnbull, *Almost French*, (Random House, 2010).

8. UNDERSTANDING FORGIVENESS

UNDERSTANDING FORGIVENESS

Forgiveness can seem challenging, sometimes even impossible as it's mixed with all sorts of misunderstandings and emotions. Here we explore what forgiveness is and is not; how it's possible to change hurtful stories about the past; what may be under our hurt; and why it's in our best interest to forgive. We'll explore simple paths to forgiveness; how to apologise; and see how doing so offers enormous benefits to our happiness and peace of mind.

Grudges Lose Their Grip Through Forgiveness

Forgiveness is often tangled up with misconceptions and emotional complexity, so let's explore its true essence and how we can weave it into daily life. **Step One** in this process involves understanding we can change our perception of past hurts through forgiveness.

Holding onto grudges and resentments, and choosing not to forgive, prevents us from living a truly happy life. In his book, *A Spiritual Renegade's Guide to the Good Life*,[1] Lama Marut suggests that, 'Holding onto grudges simply perpetuates our own suffering.'

Lama Marut suggests that our suffering stems from a fundamental misunderstanding about where both our happiness and unhappiness come from, mistakenly believing their cause comes from outside of ourselves. In reality, people, events and things do not have the power to make us happy or unhappy. Our happiness is an inside job and our responsibility. The secret to it lies in kindness and service to others, whereas holding onto unforgiveness lies counter to this.

Forgiveness involves letting go of the pain and resentment we carry from past hurts. Although it can be difficult, forgiving those who have hurt us frees us from ongoing suffering.

To begin the process of forgiveness, the first step is to believe it is possible to change our painful version of the past. Step two is to recognise that it's in our own best interests to forgive. And step three is understanding what forgiveness is and is not.

So, **Step One:** the past is changeable. The past is really only a memory of what we recall happening some time ago, brought into the present mind. For example, I remember when I was a teenager, a group of my friends went to the movies without me. I felt so hurt about being left out. This is an unpleasant memory I can hang onto and watch reruns of again and again. If allowed to go on, this can continue to disturb my present mind for years (over 50, in fact!).

It is through forgiving others that we rehabilitate or transform our hurtful memories of the past, allowing peace to arise in the present. If I can forgive my friends (the sooner the better), I can let go of the hurt I've been holding onto and live with greater contentment. In this way, it is possible to change past resentment and pain through forgiveness.

Next, we'll explore **Step Two** and why it's in our own best interests to forgive.

Forgiveness: The Ultimate Self Help Tool

Now that we know we can change our hurtful version of the past through forgiveness, we come to **Step Two:** discovering why it is in our best interest to forgive.

Trying to live a happy life while holding onto grudges and resentments is simply impractical. Marianne Williamson, in her book, *A Return to Love*,[2] asserts:

> *'Forgiveness is not always easy. At times it feels more painful than the wound we suffered, to forgive the one that inflicted it. And yet, there is no peace without forgiveness.'*

Forgiveness is not about others—it's about us. When we hold onto anger about what someone did or didn't do, and we refuse to forgive, that anger, bitterness and unhappiness sets in our minds and hearts, disturbing our peace. We may mistakenly believe that holding a grudge is easier than forgiving, but in truth, it's only through forgiveness that we can attain freedom and peace of mind.

We all operate with a degree of self-interest, so it's essential to understand that forgiveness serves our own 'enlightened self-interest.' This means recognising that we all have an innate desire and right to live a happy life, and we cannot achieve this if we are holding onto grudges and resentments.

I use these personal reminders to underscore the importance of forgiveness:

Petty annoyances can ruin our day…if we let them

If someone's actions—such as showing impatience with me while I'm doing my best to freestyle up the slow-swimming lane—annoy or upset me, I can unhelpfully hold on to that irritation for hours, disturbing my peace of mind long after my hair has dried.

A small act of forgiveness I practice is to *allow* the feeling, rather than supressing it, by doing an ABCD to Accept the feeling of annoyance. Then Breathe to Connect with my wise self, remembering I have the choice to forgive. Instead of holding onto the hurt and resentment, I choose to accept the feeling, let it go, and forgive. This is a powerful way to maintain equilibrium and prevent minor incidents from escalating into major upsets. It also means I keep turning up at the pool undaunted, which is good for my ongoing health and joy too.

Holding onto anger and resentment harms our health

Clinging to anger and resentment can have adverse effects on our physical and mental well-being, potentially leading to issues such as high blood pressure, heart problems, anxiety and stress. Connect with your wise self, and let it go.

It's never good to live or die with grudges on our conscience

In Section One we reflected on the fact that that the time of death for us all is uncertain. So while we don't know when anyone is going to die, or what happens when we die, we do know that it cannot be good to die with hatred and anger in our minds and hearts. It's important to release them and make our peace.

In our closest relationships, particularly with those we hold dear, forgiveness may prove more challenging due to the depth of emotional pain involved. Nonetheless, we can make every effort to mend fractured relationships through forgiveness, freeing ourselves from the emotional burden.

Next we'll explore **Step Three:** what forgiveness is and is not.

What Forgiveness is and is Not

The complex emotions around forgiveness lead to misconceptions and misunderstandings about what it really is. **Step Three** helps us get to the truth, assisting us in the process of practicing forgiveness.

Forgiveness is a heartfelt, reflective, emotional process, rather than a purely intellectual one. However, Lama Marut suggests that we also need to engage our intellect to understand why it's in our best interest to forgive.

Here are five things that forgiveness is not:

Forgetting

Forgiveness is not about pretending the hurt didn't happen or denying our feelings about it. It's about acknowledging and accepting the hurt and choosing a constructive response, one like forgiveness delivers.

Condoning a hurtful action

Intentionally hurting others or having others hurt us is not okay. Acknowledging and accepting the hurt is the first step towards forgiveness and helps stop the cycle of blame and retaliation. Acceptance is not apathy—it does not stop us from taking steps to protect ourselves and others or prevent future harm. Forgiveness does not mean what happened was 'okay' or that we will allow it to happen again.

Repressing the hurt

Many of us struggle to forgive because we avoid facing the very thing that hurt us—the same thing we are withholding forgiveness for. To begin the process of forgiveness, we must acknowledge and accept our feelings, then work with them kindly and compassionately.

Deciding whether the other person deserves forgiveness

Everyone deserves forgiveness, including ourselves. This is, of course, a big leap if we have been greatly harmed or abused. Forgiveness may not be the first step in such cases, as it can feel unsafe or as though we are letting the other person off the hook. The first step may be to acknowledge the hurt and recognise how unsafe we feel. In time, we can take steps toward forgiveness as a way of healing, freeing ourselves from continued suffering.

When we need to forgive ourselves, the Four Forces practice can help:

- **Refuge:** take shelter in our deeper wisdom or understanding.
- **Regret:** express sincere regret for the harmful action we have done.
- **Restraint:** make a commitment not to repeat such actions.
- **Recompense:** take positive actions to make amends. This might include forgiving ourselves or others.

Forgiveness itself can be a powerful form of Recompense. And let's not forget the fifth force, Rejoicing! Feeling glad that we have completed the first four.

Requiring the other person to apologise first:

Often others may not even be aware of or remember what they did to hurt us. Expecting an apology before we forgive can be unrealistic and keep us stuck. As Louise Hay writes in *You Can Heal Your Life*: [3]

> *'The act of forgiveness takes place in our own mind. It really has nothing to do with the other person.'*

And Nelson Mandela reminds us:

> *'Forgiveness liberates the soul. It removes fear. That is why it is such a powerful weapon.'* [4]

Let's continue to deepen our understanding of forgiveness in the next chapter.

We are Doing the Best with What We Know at the Time

Here are some tips to help us foster a more understanding perspective. Understanding helps us feel compassion for mistakes made, both by other and ourselves.

It's comforting to remember we are all doing our best with what we know at the time. But there are also reminders we can use to help us more easily embrace forgiveness, and this generates further compassion for ourselves and others.

The most effective reminders for me are:

- Realising that it's in our own best interest to forgive.

- Remembering the truth of connection and thus avoiding disconnection.

- Acknowledging that it's through making mistakes, we learn. Take Albert Einstein's quote into consideration: 'A person who never made a mistake never tried anything new'. [5]

- Understanding that happy people are rarely interested in hurting others.

Thich Nhat Hanh writes in *Peace is Every Step: The Path of Mindfulness in Everyday life,* [6]

> *'When another person makes you suffer it is because they suffer deeply within himself or herself. And his or her suffering is spilling over. He or she does not need punishment; he or she needs help—that is the message he or she is sending by hurting you. So have compassion for them. That is the human response to someone who is hurting and therefore needing to hurt others'.*

I relate deeply to Thich Nhat Hanh's words. Happy people are rarely interested in hurting others. Sadly, unhappy people hurt both others and themselves. I've noticed when I'm happy, I'm not interested in causing harm, but when I'm unhappy or needy, I can lash out. Since we all share similar tendencies at different stages in this regard, we can cultivate more understanding and compassion toward each other.

We are all doing our best, with what we know at the time, is a comforting reminder we are all in it together.

It's also comforting to understand what lies beneath our hurt so we can deal with it. That's what the next chapter covers.

What Lies Beneath Hurt?

Embracing forgiveness involves taking a closer look into why we are hurt, and understanding what lies beneath both the small hurts, and larger wounds.

For me, deepening my understanding of forgiveness, and putting it into practice, has brought benefits to my happiness and peace of mind. In this reflection, we will look more deeply into what may be underneath our hurt, particularly in relation to those we are closest to. When I'm brave enough, I've found it's helpful to look at what is at the root of my hurt, as this allows me to understand my reactions to the small things and the deeper hurts too.

Deep Relationship Understandings:

We've likely all experienced deep, close, relationship hurts. I realise I feel such particular pain in this area because these relationships are important to me and I care what those closest to me think. For me, my parents were a great place to explore this. I have many unhelpful storylines related to my parents' shortcomings, and instances I've felt hurt and let down. This blame and criticism builds resentment, making me unhappy and disturbing my peace of mind.

I can remember feeling upset and hurt when, after finishing my university course and during my graduation, I perceived my father was uninterested in my achievements. When I am able to look back at this, I can see this was about my unmet needs—I was seeking love, approval and support from him. I realise now that by recognising and acknowledging this unfulfilled need I am in a position to be able provide this love, approval and support for myself (and my kids) rather than continuing to feel upset at my father for not providing it for me.

My ABCD practice helped too: Accepting the feeling of hurt, Breathing, Connecting with my wise self to Do—to give myself what I need—in this case love and approval. In addition, I can seek this support from someone in a position more able to give it—like my brother.

Holding onto grudges and resentments about my parents also stops me from appreciating the incredible things they did do, such as giving me many opportunities. It's so easy to concentrate on the negatives, with blame, criticism, hurt, and resentment. When I tune into my wise self, I am reminded that it's best to acknowledge and accept the hurt and choose to release it through forgiveness, giving more space to focus on gratitude. As always, being grateful helps everything.

Grasping onto big hurts and grudges also takes a huge amount of emotional and physical energy, disturbing our peace of mind and happiness. Repairing these relationships through forgiveness is possible and necessary, and while it may take time, is aways beneficial.

We'll discuss the process of staying connected through forgiveness next.

Maybe you have someone who comes to mind now, someone whom it's time to forgive?

Keep Connection Through Forgiveness

Rather than disconnecting when something goes wrong, it's more helpful to remain connected and learn to forgive.

It is so easy to disconnect from others when we feel hurt by them. But we can heal this disconnection through forgiveness. I've found it helpful to understand that beneath my anger and hurt can sometimes be a deeper feeling of not being respected.

When I feel this lack of respect—or lack of appreciation or love—my habitual reaction can be to disconnect, blame and criticise. Thoughts like on being tooted in traffic, 'Stupid impatient woman. I'm doing nothing wrong. How dare she!' are examples of my outrage. Of course, this never helps and only creates more separation and hurt.

Staying connected and forgiving can better mend the divisions we feel. Sometimes, we are even in danger of disconnecting from ourselves. We can be a critical, harsh, and unforgiving taskmaster instead of being our own kind, encouraging friend.

Forgiveness opens the heart, helping us find connection again. It releases the hurt, replacing it with love and happiness.

It's important to remember though, that forgiveness does not mean we have to be friends with the person, or that they need to know we have forgiven them, or that we will allow ourselves to be hurt again.

So, when that testing teenager criticises me and I am tempted to criticise back, creating even more disconnection, I find it helpful to pause and remember to be kind to all involved. I use my internal 'please be kind' reminder as a full stop, preventing me from reacting harshly and allowing for healing through forgiveness.

Simply thinking, 'I forgive you' to myself', keeps this important connection.

In the next chapter we'll look at other causes of disconnection.

Blame and Criticism, The Great Disconnectors

Blame and criticism can hinder growth and connection.

Watching Simon Sinek's memorable YouTube video on *Millennials in the Workplace* [7] I was reminded how unhelpful it can be to blame and criticise our parents, something which I have indulged in in the past. And as a parent myself, being on the receiving end of this criticism, I can now appreciate how it feels! The video also served as a beautiful reminder that it's never helpful to blame, criticise and refuse to forgive, whether as offspring, parents, friends, or in any relationship.

Often beneath our feelings of hurt, anger, abandonment, or being let down is something deeper. I find it helpful to understand that beneath each of those feelings is my outraged ego, standing with its hands on its hips, blowing things out of proportion, saying something like:

- You don't respect me.
- You don't love me enough.
- You don't appreciate me.
- You don't hear or see me.

And even though these thoughts are only in my head, and aren't necessarily true, if I do believe them to be true, I disconnect.

Another person's anger often has nothing to do with me at all, but is about what's going on for them and in their life. But, when I feel this lack of respect, appreciation, love, or not being listened to, supported, or approved of, my habitual reaction can be to disconnect from that person. This, of course, creates even more separation and hurt.

When I disconnect, I:

- Deny my own feelings.
- Put up walls to shut out both my emotions and the other person.
- Resort to blaming and criticising them, with all the 'nevers' and 'shoulds,' using phrases like: 'you *never* help me', 'you *never* thank me', 'you *should* pay me more respect', 'you *should* listen to me', or 'you *should* do what I say'.
- Build up my case of hurt and resentment against them with storylines of blame.

There are ways to handle this so much more helpfully and we'll learn how in the next reflection.

Forgiveness Connects

Forgiveness fosters a more positive, happy, and connected reality. Let's talk healing and growth.

When we deny our emotions, fall into blame or criticism, or build a case against others—without offering forgiveness to them or to ourselves—our relationships and inner peace suffer. Forgiveness, by contrast, helps preserve connection and is essential for our well-being, peace of mind, and happiness.

So instead of disconnecting, we can:

- Recognise negative patterns when they arise and tune into our wise self to replace them with something more positive and encouraging. This will create a more positive, happy, and connected reality.
- Practice forgiveness on the spot as we go about our day. This serves as a reminder not to disconnect—from others or ourselves.
- Be kind and encouraging to everyone, including yourself.
- Apologise, when necessary.
- Forgive, both yourself and others.

Placing the emphasis on forgiveness, we can:

- *Allow* and Accept your emotions, then work with them.
- Understand that it is in our own self-interest to forgive, bringing us the peace and freedom we want and deserve.
- Forgive not only the surface hurts but also what is underneath the hurt, no matter how big or small.
- Realise that we don't want to disconnect, but our deeper wish is to find the truth of connection.
- Remember that we all make mistakes, it's how we learn.

When forgiving the mistakes of others and ourselves, consider this wisdom from Malcolm X:

> 'Don't be in such a hurry to condemn a person because he does not do what you do or think as you think. There was a time you didn't know what you know now.' [8]

Others have their reasons for doing what they do and we can all act from a place of misunderstanding. It's better for our peace of mind to allow others the freedom to act as they must and forgive them for any feelings of hurt, anger, or abandonment. Trying to overly control other people just brings us more suffering and disconnection.

Disconnection also arises when we try to bypass our feelings and we'll explore that next.

Beware of Bypassing Feelings

Let's deepen our understanding of forgiveness and explore how to avoid the pitfalls of bypassing negative emotions.

Bypassing is when we ignore or suppress uncomfortable emotions rather than directly addressing them. This can leave unresolved feelings bubbling beneath, which may arise in unexpected or harmful ways.

Alongside this, we may notice a critical voice in our heads – the one that protests and insists we *shouldn't* forgive. Rather than trying to bypass, ignore, or silence that voice, I've found it far more helpful to acknowledge it with a simple, 'Thank you for sharing your view.' When it feels heard, it quiets down, allowing me to check in with my wiser self and ask what to do next. And more often than not, the answer is forgiveness.

Forgiveness acknowledges the feelings of hurt or wrongdoing and embarks on a process of releasing them out of a desire for peace of mind and closure. So whereas bypassing avoids, forgiveness heals.

We cannot heal until we feel—meaning we need to *feel* the hurt to be able to *forgive* the hurt. That's why our first step is to be aware, to acknowledge the feelings of hurt, and have compassion toward ourselves first.

Forgiveness is **not** about pretending something did not happen or condoning the behaviour, forgetting and failing to learn from it, or re-running the hurt and blame soundtrack in our mind.

But forgiveness is about getting in touch with the truth of our hurt and identifying who or what has hurt us, so we can process the emotions and work towards forgiving others and ourselves.

As we will discover later through the concept of All Day Forgiveness, if we continually exercise our forgiveness and apology muscles on the small things, we are better prepared for the bigger hurts—including forgiving those we are closest to and forgiving ourselves.

That's what the following reflections will help us do.

Apologising

Now let's talk about the power of apologising as a way to humble ourselves and work towards forgiveness. Though it can be difficult, it's necessary to maintain connection and grow compassion.

By apologising to others when we've done something we're not happy about, we not only humble ourselves, but work towards developing compassion for ourselves and others, paving the way for forgiveness and connection. A lot of our inability to forgive comes from pride or judgment. Statements such as, 'How dare they do that to me?' are common.

Take for example when I was tooted at traffic lights, maybe I did take too long after the light turned green, or perhaps the woman tooting her horn had somewhere to be urgently. Who knows? But what I do know is that I blamed and criticised her. Instead, apologising and forgiving would have worked much better for my peace of mind. As with forgiveness, we can start by apologising for the small, everyday hurts which also helps us build our muscles to deal with deeper ones.

Apologising does not always mean that you are wrong and the other person is right. It can mean that you value your relationship more than your ego. I experienced this when a person I am close to felt very hurt by my behaviour. I felt that I could not control the situation that caused the hurt and was in an impossible situation. The person told me they no longer wanted a relationship with me. I valued this relationship and was able to genuinely apologise for the hurt I had caused. I was truly sorry and thankfully, this apology kept us connected for many years to come.

When appropriate, it is usually most helpful to apologise to others face-to-face. Sometimes forming this connection in person can be beneficial, but sometimes it is not possible or appropriate. In those cases, it's still helpful to apologise mentally, in our minds. Sometimes, an apology might cause the other person distress, shame, or be perceived as insincere and a 'goody two shoes act' on your behalf. We need to consider what's best for the other person too, even if we're eager to unburden ourselves. Regardless, we can still rest in the kind intention of being regretful—no matter what happens.

A personal word of warning regarding the phrase 'I'm sorry'. As a teenager, I developed an unhelpful habit of saying 'I'm sorry' that extended to just about everything. I am sure it was annoying for everyone, but looking back, I feel compassion for my younger self. She clearly felt as though she was always in the wrong—like she was a bother or taking up too much space—probably a habit which developed as a young child, when she was trying to be liked, fit in, and a good girl. Noticing this unhelpful tendency has helped me develop more appropriate ways to offer genuine apologies when truly needed.

One way to turn around our habit of over-apologising is to use 'thank you' instead of (or as well as) apologising. So, in a situation where you might be late for an appointment, instead of saying, 'I'm so sorry, I'm late', you could instead express, 'thank you for your patience and for waiting for me'. You may find this interesting to try in some situations and notice how the interaction shifts or the connection strengthens.

Ultimately, as the saying goes, 'the best apology is changed behaviour'. If we're truly sorry for our actions, we make amends with an apology but also commit to a resolution to not repeat the hurtful behaviour. This is yet another application of the 'Four Forces': Refuge in our understanding of causality, Regret over our actions, Restraint from the misdeed, and Recompense through apology and changed behaviour.

There are countless reasons why it's in our best interest to forgive and also to apologise. By bringing *awareness*, strength, logic and compassion to the process it becomes easier too. I hope you are fired up to forgive the small everyday things and enthused to practice appropriate apologies. Remember to do your best, with kindness and compassion for everyone—including yourself.

Next we cover ways to forgive.

How To Forgive

Understanding the suffering behind others' actions can aid us in practicing forgiveness. We can mindfully face the hurt, breathe, and offer forgiveness in contemplation.

Recognising that unhappy people are suffering, and that this suffering is often why they hurt others, fosters both compassion and forgiveness. It allows us to have compassion toward others and their mistakes, as well as toward our own. Forgiveness is how we heal, which is why it's so important to learn *how* to.

So, how do we forgive? Lama Marut taught this method:

- Sit, close your eyes, and bring to mind the person who hurt you. You might picture them sitting in front of you.
- *Allow* and Accept the feeling that arises: acknowledge the hurt, abandonment, or anger.
- Breathe mindfully.
- In your mind, say to this person, 'I forgive you unconditionally', repeating this for as long as you feel necessary.
- Repeat this process daily, for as long and as many times as you feel the need.

I have practiced this contemplation many times, especially when dealing with the big hurts. It is a process, and often, just when I think I am done, I feel the need to repeat it. But I can happily say that during our family Christmas get-togethers these days, I have a much more helpful and kind soundtrack playing in my head. Through forgiveness, I have let go of much of the blame, criticism, and hurt, and instead am able to be more compassionate, kind, and appreciative to all, including myself.

Maybe you feel motivated to deepen your forgiveness practice by extending that kindness and compassion toward yourself now too.

There are ideas for starting with forgiveness for small hurts next.

Begin by Forgiving Minor Hurts

Forgiving minor hurts is a wonderful way to exercise our 'forgiveness muscles'. We can do this through using the ABCD method to prevent the accumulation of minor irritations that can disrupt our inner peace.

A good way to begin exercising our forgiveness muscles is by addressing the small hurts. Our ABCD method helps us work through feelings such as hurt or anger, rather than holding onto them with bitterness and resentment.

For instance, when that person in the slow swimming lane says tersely, 'I need to go first, because I am faster than you', and I feel the sting of my wounded pride, I try to remind myself to use the four-step ABCD practice instead of ruining my swim with anger.

I do this by:

- Maintaining *awareness* of the triggered emotion and Accept that anger is occurring. I might think 'Ouch, my swimming pride is hurt', which helps me avoid suppressing or inappropriately expressing my irritation.

- I then take a deep Breath to Connect with my wise self for guidance on what to do next.

- Once the next steps are clearer, I can take action and Do what I intuitively feel is more beneficial. This might include talking with someone I trust, safely expressing my feelings, kindly communicating my hurt to the person involved, or—as is the case with minor hurts—letting go and forgiving.

It often feels right to offer forgiveness in my mind, silently saying 'I forgive you', without expressing it outwardly. If I were to say it aloud, I might find there is more forgiveness work to do, because of the other person's reaction.

Martin Luther King Jr. said, 'Forgiveness is not an occasional act; it is a constant attitude'. [9] This describes a practice of 'All Day Forgiveness', it's about forgiving minor hurts on the spot, as they happen and helps prevent little annoyances from building up and ruining our peace of mind.

Let's explore All Day Forgiveness next.

All Day Forgiveness

All Day Forgiveness promotes constant emotional awareness, wise reactions, and resilience, helping us foster inner peace and harmony.

Forgiveness can be transformative, even in small everyday situations, helping to prevent minor annoyances from building up and ruining the whole day.

An All Day Forgiveness Experience

Recently, I had an interesting reminder of the importance of kindness and All Day Forgiveness. I made a trip to the supermarket to buy socks to donate to Sacred Heart Mission. There was a two-for-one deal on some socks, but when I got to the cash register, the checkout discount did not appear.

I sought help from a staff member, someone I've experienced being grumpy at times. She became frustrated, muttering under her breath tersely. I could feel my own annoyance arise in response to her rudeness, so took a breath and checked in with my wise self to be reminded that I had no idea what was going on for her. I chose to be kind.

Gently, I said to the staff member, 'Please be kind' (something I remember saying to my teenage kids many times). She gave an exasperated sigh. But to my surprise, I then noticed the label on the socks which read: 'It feels good to be kind'. The message felt like a perfect reminder at the perfect time. I said to myself 'I forgive you'.

By practicing All Day Forgiveness, I was able to leave the supermarket feeling lighter, more forgiving of her frustration and grateful for the unexpected affirmation of kindness.

The next day, I saw the same staff member. She came up to me and said, 'I'm sorry I was so frustrated with you; I have a lot going on.' I told her I understood she had a very demanding job and thanked her for her apology.

Because I had practiced All Day Forgiveness the previous day, I had no build-up of resentment. Generating a more forgiving heart toward others, and toward myself and my own reactions, has helped me release the tension of holding onto small hurts. This practice builds my emotional awareness and resilience, so I'm less likely to 'sweat the small stuff'.

It's important to forgive ourselves too and we cover this in the next reflection.

Self-Forgiveness

Self-forgiveness is often overlooked, yet it plays a crucial role in healing. This reflection offers a personal example of how to practice forgiving ourselves.

We've covered the importance of forgiving and apologising to others, but just as important is the ability to forgive ourselves.

I am sure I hurt my mother when I was a teenager, and I regret the feelings of rejection and sadness I caused her. Likely stemming from my insecurities and low self-confidence, I felt embarrassed by her, purposely left her out of things and didn't share what was going on in my life. So, in this instance, it is that insecure, under-confident teenage Maree I want to forgive. She was doing the best she could back then, lacking the wisdom and tools that the present me has available.

Here's how I forgive my teenage self by using Lama Marut's method:

- I sit, close my eyes and bring teenage Maree to mind. I picture her with her long hair and hippy dress from Ishka.

- I allow and Accept the feelings that arise; acknowledging the guilt, anger, uncertainty and the need for approval and to fit in.

- I Breathe mindfully

- In my mind, I say to teenage Maree 'I forgive you unconditionally', repeating this for as long as I need to
- I repeat this process daily, as many times as I feel necessary, for as long as I feel necessary

I've found Lama Marut's self forgiveness mantra so useful, and have also been changed by an ancient Hawaiian mantra which helps with the same. It's up next for you.

Ho'oponopono Self Forgiveness Mantra

Forgiving ourselves can sometimes be more challenging than forgiving others. Explore the powerful *Ho'oponopono* practice, an ancient Hawaiian mantra for self-forgiveness and healing that cultivates inner peace and happiness.

A self-forgiveness practice I learned some years ago and have found extremely useful is *Ho'oponopono*, an ancient Hawaiian practice of reconciliation and forgiveness.

Ho'oponopono

This ancient Hawaiian Mantra has been used by the Kahuna, mystic healers, for centuries. We can use it to heal the relationship with ourselves or to release a painful memory.

The practice takes place in our minds.

Close your eyes and repeat these four phrases with prayerful intention:

- I'm sorry
- Please forgive me
- Thank you
- I love you

When saying these four phrases, be sincere, mean them and open yourself to their power. As this is the last reflection in the Forgiveness chapter, I invite you to do this guided practice now:

I'm sorry: Apologising or repenting

- We understand that apologising is important for our peace of mind and acknowledge any hurt we have caused ourselves.
- We can say to ourselves, 'I am sorry for...,' things like judging you; punishing you; speaking harshly to you; comparing you to others; believing you weren't good enough; criticising you; pushing you too hard; not letting you rest; not being patient...say whatever comes up for you.
- Say each phrase, i.e., 'I'm sorry for...', and exhale, as you say what you are sorry for.

Please forgive me: Asking for forgiveness

- Next, we seek forgiveness, which is essential for our healing.
- We can say to ourselves, 'Please forgive me for...', things like judging you; punishing you; comparing you to others; speaking harshly to you; believing you weren't good enough; criticising you; pushing you too hard; not letting you rest; not being patient... whatever comes up for you.
- Say each phrase, i.e., 'Please forgive me for...', exhale as you say what you are asking forgiveness for.

Thank you: Giving appreciation

- Gratitude is so important for our well-being.
- So, we can say to ourselves, 'Thank you for...', things like always being there for me; guiding me; knowing me; listening to me; loving me... whatever comes up for you.
- Say each phrase, i.e., 'Thank you for...', exhale as you reflect on what you are thankful for.

I love you: Feeling love

- There is nothing as powerful as love.
- In this final step, we say to ourselves, 'I love you...', and think of things like loving all of you; loving yourself unconditionally; loving you warts and all; loving and accepting you even when you are feeling sad, angry or whatever you are feeling; loving everything you have been; loving everything you will be.

Allow the breath to help you release all the tension. Rest in any feeling you have of peace, love and contentment.

I hope you found that helpful. When you're ready, we can add the power of the Four Forces. Ideas for this follow.

The Four Forces as a Path to Forgiveness

We've all made mistakes, but dwelling on guilt is unhelpful. The Four Forces practice, akin to 'mind gardening,' offers a path to self-forgiveness, self-compassion, and positive growth.

I remember making things difficult for a waiter one night by changing my order four times. The waiter became short with me, made a critical comment and I served another one back. Endlessly feeling guilty about it and bashing myself up with negative self-talk though wouldn't help me learn from the situation or help the person I'd hurt.

The Four Forces practice (previously outlined in Section 3: 'Foundational Practices' on page 81), can help us practice forgiveness. The practice is a bit like 'mind gardening' and useful for clearing our conscience and letting go of unhelpful guilt.

The Four Forces applied to forgiveness:

- **Recognise** what happened and admit it: Yes, I did it. I got angry and responded with criticism.

- **Refuge:** Acting like this and not considering others is not making me happy, nor is it helping me be the positive, happy force I want to be.

- **Regret:** Good healthy regret. I wish I hadn't snapped back angrily.

- **Restraint:** I will restrain from responding with criticism for the next week. Each time I feel criticised, I will try to be aware my 'criticism button' is being pushed. I'll try to *allow* and **A**ccept the feeling of frustration, **B**reathe, and **C**onnect to my wise self to respond more wisely.

- **Recompense:** Forgiveness of others and ourselves can be wonderful recompense activities. These make-up activities help make amends for both the hurt caused by the waiter's behaviour, and my retaliatory criticism. I chose to forgive them for criticising me and to apologise to them for my outburst. Who knows what they had going on in their life or other customers' and manager's demands at the restaurant that night? I also learned to be more confident in my decision-making when ordering.

It is important to forgive the person who we feel hurt by and to forgive ourselves for our reaction, rather than continue to give ourselves a hard time. Apologising and forgiving both others and ourselves can be wonderful ways to make amends.

- **Rejoice:** Feel really happy about doing the Four Forces Practice, especially for following through on recompense and forgiveness. Instead of letting this incident ruin my day, I happily moved on, having forgiven both myself and the other person. We can also practice All-day Forgiveness with these small, everyday hurts too.

Given this is the final reflection in this section, please join me in rejoicing in the fact that we and others have read, contemplated or practiced these practices and reflections to foster our understanding of forgiveness.

Maybe you would like to

- Rewrite a hurtful story from your past. Maybe you could bring to mind some minor hurt you have been holding onto and try reframing them in a more compassionate way.
- Make a note about why it is in your best interest to forgive.
- Spend some time contemplating what forgiveness is and is not and how an on-the-go practice of forgiveness might halt the build-up of hurt and resentment.
- Think of someone you would like to forgive and try to bring some understanding to the notion that they may be suffering, or doing the best with what they know at the time.
- Be aware of the temptation we all have to bypass our feelings by attempting to suppress or ignore them. Instead, try to accept and feel them, allowing them to pass.

- Be aware of that critical voice in your head, the one that may be protesting about not forgiving, or giving you a hard time in some way. Instead of trying to banish that critical voice, have a go at accepting it with a 'thank you for sharing your views'. This allows for it to feel heard. End the discussion there and then check in with the wise self for what to do, which may include to forgive.

- Think of something you regret doing and that you would like to apologise for. Start with something small and do it in person or as a mental practice—whatever you feel is best.

- Choose someone you would like to forgive. It may be best to start small, use Lama Marut's forgiveness practice.

- Have fun with an all-day forgiveness practice. Maybe just start being mindful of forgiving little hurts for a few hours during the day. Include forgiving yourself too!

- Do a Four Forces practice on something you regret doing, using forgiveness of yourself or others as the Recompense.

- Try the *Ho'oponopono* Self Forgiveness Mantra

Let's feel glad for all the positive energy we have created together and dedicate this to the happiness and wellbeing of all.

And now it's onto the final section, it's all about kindness—how being kind to both ourselves and others paves the way to true happiness— it's a lovely way to end.

Step One: We can Change past hurts

1. Lama Marut, *A Spiritual Renegades Guide to the Good Life*, (Atria, Simon and Schuster 2012).

Step Two; Why it's important to forgive

2. Marianne, Williamson, *A Return to Love*, (Harper Collins 1996).

Forgiveness understandings

3. Louise Hay, *You Can Heal Your Life*, (Hay House, 1999).

4. Nelson Mandala, https://quotefancy.com/quote/874257/Nelson-Mandela-Forgiveness-liberates-the-soul-It-removes-fear-That-is-why-it-is-such-a

5. Albert Einstein, *Einstein Quotes*: http://www.alberteinsteinsite.com/quotes/einsteinquotes.html

6. Thich Nhat Hanh, *Peace is Every Step: The Path of Mindfulness in Everyday life*, (Bantom Books, 1982).

Millennials in the workplace

7. Simon Sinek, *Millennials in the Workplace*, You Tube: https://www.youtube.com/watch?v=hERoQp6QJNU

Be compassionate to the suffering of others

8. Malcolm X, *Goodreads Quotes*: https://www.goodreads.com/quotes/281078-don-t-be-in-a-hurry-to-condemn-because-he-doesn-t

9. Martin Luther King Jr., *Goodreads Quotes*: https://www.goodreads.com/quotes/57037-forgiveness-is-not-an-occasional-act-it-is-a-constant

9. KINDNESS TO ALL

(Including Ourselves)

KINDNESS TO ALL

Open the door to happiness by being kind to others and ourselves. Kindness has a profound and lasting effect on everyone so we will explore ways to be less judgmental; encourage a positive outlook; be kinder and more compassionate; and create kind boundaries to prevent harm. We will also explore other hacks to be kinder; tuning into our internal intuitive wisdom to be kind and encouraging and to befriend those inner dragons.

Kindness: The Key to Happiness

As the Dalai Lama says, kindness is simple yet profound. Research also reveals it is the key to happiness. Being mindful of our intention to be compassionate and kind benefits us all immensely.

The Dalai Lama says, 'My religion is very simple. My religion is kindness'. [1]

Kindness makes a huge difference to how we feel about ourselves, others and our lives. Research shows that when we act kindly, the same parts of the brain light up as they do when we receive a reward—like money, or even chocolate!

True happiness can be experienced when we are mindfully kind, grateful and compassionate; and especially when the giving is done without expectation of something in return.

I think we've all likely felt the lovely lift in spirits when we connect with others through kindness. It's one of the greatest gifts we can offer, and, as the saying goes: is a gift everyone can afford to give.

We often do kind, generous things throughout the day without noticing, but it's helpful to bring mindful awareness to these times, no matter how small. For example, a smile can totally change someone's day for the better. It also brightens our day when we notice the kindness of others and feel happy about it. Doing anonymous acts of kindness is especially fun and powerful because it removes the self-interest from our actions.

There are many fun ways to do this, including paying for someone's coffee or picking up a neighbour's bin that's fallen over in the street.

Sometimes, our kindness may need to be strong. For example, as a parent, we can say 'No' to our children in a firm voice, with the kind intention of preventing harm, to themselves or others. Our kind intention matters. We'll explore this more in the upcoming reflections on setting kind boundaries.

Because we are all interconnected, every situation and person offers the opportunity to practice kindness. And because we develop a more positive, happy perception of ourselves when we show kindness to others, we can therefore be grateful to others for this opportunity too.

Paradoxically, whether we make others happy isn't up to us—it is up to them. For instance, if we have a kind intention and offer someone a seat on the train, it can be met with thanks, indifference or maybe even hostility.

Sometimes I forget I don't have the power to make someone happy, so when my kindness doesn't seem to be appreciated, I am thrown for a loop. But when I am mindful of my intention to be kind, I create the causes for a happier perception of myself. An analogy I find helpful is this: we can prepare a beautiful banquet for others to enjoy, but whether they choose to partake is not up to us, it's up to them.

What really helps me is resting in my kind intention. When I do that, I no longer feel the need to justify myself or blame others for how they react.

For example, when someone was angry with me for being late—even though circumstances beyond my control caused the delay—I reminded myself of my kind intention to be on time. That helped me avoid becoming defensive, over-explaining, or trying to justify myself with excuses. Defensiveness often turns into a game of criticism ping pong, when a simple 'thank-you for your patience' or apology may be the best course of action.

Remembering these things helps motivate me to be a positive, kind force in the world. In my day-to-day life, this means I ask: 'Who could benefit from my support, encouragement, and kindness?' And, what do you know, suddenly people (including myself!) start popping into my awareness reminding me there are wonderful opportunities to practice kindness right where we are.

Sometimes, thinking about all those in need can feel overwhelming though and when I feel this, I try to remember, 'Peace begins with me' and 'Act local and think global', and then I can see that kindness doesn't need to be big or expensive. A simple kind word or gentle smile can make a difference. I am constantly reminded that kindness is a wonderful way to connect.

Kindness to all includes kindness to you too It's equally as important to be kind to yourself as well as others. We'll talk more about this in the upcoming reflections.

Kindness Can Have a Profound, Lasting Effect

Let's explore the lasting impact kindness can have on our self-perception and the importance of extending it to others.

American lawyer and writer Robert Ingersoll says, 'We rise by lifting others.' [2] This resonates deeply with me. We all know how good it feels to compliment and encourage others, just as we know the uplift felt on receiving kindness and encouragement ourselves. We all have many opportunities to do this yet often underestimate the power of kindness and its ability to shape our lives and our self-perception in profound ways.

I'm reminded of two school teachers who hugely influenced my life through their encouragement and kindness. One was my Year 12 biology teacher, who assured me I would pass with flying colours, even when I was new to biology and greatly doubted my abilities. I often remember her kind encouragement when I lacked the courage to try something hard.

Similarly, my Year 3 teacher gave kind reassurance when I was unsure. I still fondly remember class rest time when we would lay our heads on our folded arms at our desks. Even now, when we do a similar pose in yoga class, I'm transported back to this teacher and Year 3 rest time when I felt that kind, safe energy she created.

It's likely these teachers would be unaware of the profound effect their kindness had on my life and that I'm so grateful for their encouragement. We all have the ability to offer this gift to others in all sorts of ways, both big and small.

Remember too, to rejoice in the ways you are a kind, positive force in the world. Encouraging yourself to keep it up helps strengthen a positive self-perception, further inspiring you to keep spreading kindness. As with my teachers, the ripple-effect is immeasurable.

Let's be inspired by kind, encouraging people like these and the others you come across. And be kind and encouraging to ourselves too, knowing this can have a life-changing effect on all. Another thing that can be life-changing is regarding the voices you choose to listen to. That's coming up next.

Positive Polly or Negative Nelly?

Do you get caught up in negative thinking? It's easy to slip into, but it's not kind to ourselves or others to do so. With awareness, we can change our mindset and cultivate more kindness and positivity.

Thinking negatively can become a habit that drags us down into gloom and doom, but thankfully, it's a habit we can change through *awareness*. By becoming mindful of unhelpful negative thinking and opening ourselves up to more positive and optimistic ways of thinking, our perspective on life gets a fantastic boost.

Have you ever been around people who put a pessimistic spin on everything or are caught in a loop of complaints, stuck in a seemingly hopeless, unchangeable mindset? I've experienced this with a friend who was deeply unhappy with her living situation and not yet open to change the narrative or make alternative choices.

Rather than getting swept up in negativity or responding with blame and criticism, I tried to meet her and her unhelpful thinking with more compassion.

After all, being stuck in a noisy complaint loop with no idea how to change the situation is no fun.

While tempted to say, 'Stop being so negative, focus on the positive,' I knew this would inflame the situation. A kinder, positive, empathetic response was required. I watched one of my other friends skillfully, playfully and kindly say, 'I understand it's difficult; come on, Negative Nelly, let's find Positive Polly in there.' Her acknowledgement that the situation was hard, combined with her levity, lightened everything up and we were soon laughing.

We can all find ourselves in that unhelpful spot of negativity, but with *awareness*, we can also get ourselves out of it! This is not about pretending there aren't any difficulties; certainly, things can be tricky at times. Nor is it about bypassing or repressing our feelings. Instead, we can rely on our trusty ABCD: Accepting our feelings, taking a Breath and Connecting with our wise selves on what to Do—how to best respond with kindness when things don't go as planned.

My friend's actions that day reminded me we can all choose to bring our Positive Polly, Sunny Sam or Optimistic Oli voices and approach to any situation.

In the next chapter we'll discuss how kindness sometimes benefits from setting compassionate boundaries too.

Kindness with a Backbone

Kindness makes a difference—but so do compassionate boundaries.

I'm often reminded of the impact we can have through even the smallest acts of kindness. I know how good it feels to be on the receiving end of an eye twinke, an offer of help, an encouraging word or a compliment, and it feels equally good to offer this to others, too. This is the energy I want to be around and the kind I try to bring with me.

And yet, life isn't always lived in this happy space. Sometimes we and those around us are just not in a position to be kind or positive. While it's important to be compassionate and understanding about this, if someone's suffering leads them to act out with anger or aggression, setting a compassionate boundary can be the kindest response of all necessary to protect both ourselves and others from harm.

This quote from Maya Angelou reminds me that we are all doing the best with what we know at the time, but that does not let us off the hook when it comes to taking responsibility for our behaviour. She says, 'Do the best you can until you know better. Then when you know better, do better.' [3]

When someone is being hurtful or unkind, the kindest thing we can do is to put a boundary in place with compassion.

I'm becoming better at asking my wise self for guidance on setting these boundaries. Whether it's saying, 'I'm finding your behaviour hurtful and I need to leave now,' or 'Please be kind', this boundary setting is an act of kindness for both myself and the other person, avoiding further harm.

Here are some other ways to set boundaries:

- When others are gossiping, being negative, catastrophising, or talking about things you find distressing, it may be helpful to remove yourself from that environment. Any truthful excuse will do. 'Sorry, I need to go' with no need to explain is often all that's required.

- While it may be compassionate to lend a kind, empathetic ear to someone in need, it's not necessarily helpful to let them go on and on with a gloom and doom monologue or endless negativity loop. Sometimes offering, 'I hear what you say, that must be difficult' or 'yes, you've told me you don't like that' acknowledges their distress but doesn't feed into the narrative.

- It's helpful to be diplomatic when offering help; recognising when someone does not want our assistance, or to help themselves. In these situations, if the person just wants to repeat the story (particularly if we have heard it many times) and we can see they are stuck in the story—it may be appropriate to kindly relay that you understand, but have heard it before and that they may find it helpful to seek more appropriate support.

- Sometimes boundaries are disrupted, like when someone invades our personal space, disrespects our need for privacy, uses hurtful or abusive language or makes a request we are unable to or not comfortable to meet. In these situations, we can give ourselves kind boundaries, such as choosing not to engage, especially when someone is trying to hurt or rile us up, physically removing ourselves by moving away, actively putting a hand up to say something like 'please don't speak to me like that' or 'please respect my privacy'. Saying 'no' when it is not in our best interest to engage in a situation or to meet a request is another boundary. This boundary setting is an act of kindness for both themselves and you.

- My friend Lorraine talks about boundaries as being like 'a yellow raincoat' that we put on so that hurtful comments just run right off. This reminds me to stay kind and not take things so personally.

So, be a spreader of positivity, joy, and kindness, while also using boundaries as needed. And remember, even the tiniest gestures of kindness and positivity toward yourself and others will have a remarkable positive effect. Less judgement also leads to great outcomes so we'll cover that next.

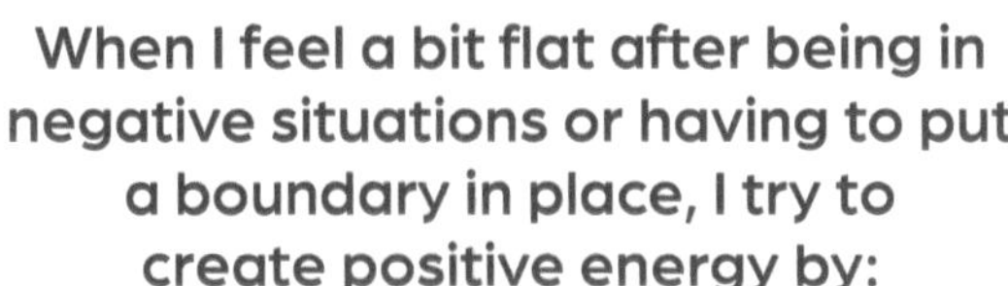

- Listening to music and singing (especially in the car on my way home from visiting a grumpy relative!)
- Dancing
- Running/walking
- Taking a shower
- Smiling
- Laughing
- Reading something uplifting
- Speaking kindly and encouragingly to myself
- Consoling a friend
- Standing for a cause such as giving my support to others who are in a compromised or disadvantaged situation
- Getting out in nature
- Feeling inspired

More Kindness, Less Judgement

When navigating hurtful behaviors and quick judgments, I strive to practice kindness and embrace empathy for myself and others. You can too!

Sometimes when I experience others behaving in hurtful ways it can be challenging to release my judgement of them or let go of my sense of victimhood. But I continue to try to and have found the following helpful:

- Consider that this person is giving me opportunities to practice kindness and compassion, of course toward my own feelings but also toward the person I am feeling hurt by.

- The anonymous quote: '*You never know what someone is dealing with behind closed doors. No matter how happy someone looks, how loud their laugh, or how big their smile, there can always be a level of indescribable hurt*', describes how things are often far more complex than what they appear to be. This reminds me to be kind and compassionate, even —and especially— when others cannot.

- I often assume I know what is going on with others and this quick judgment is not helpful. My friend Ali reminded me of the old saying: 'When we *ASSUME*, we make an *ASS* of *U* and *ME*'. It brings me needed clarity when I'm quick to judge, such as when I slap a label on someone just based on how they look. If we can interrupt these assumptions, we can pay closer attention to others and become curious about their reality; for instance, perhaps their clothing expresses something important to them, or perhaps what they wear just isn't a priority.

- Rather than judge myself for this human tendency to assume, label and judge, I instead try to move forward with kindness and curiosity. I often hear my wise self remind me: 'My funny mind, look what it's judging now, I have no need to judge myself or others.'

With more focus on kindness and less on judgment, I also try to remember to do the following simple things:

- Choosing to be kind in many small ways: with compliments, deeds to help, friendly texts, smiles, listening with a kind, empathic ear. And to do these things without waiting for recognition or a thank you. True kindness is giving without the expectation of something in return. Remember, you can always thank yourself for being a positive force in the world.

- I offer myself the affirmation: 'I am Loved, Appreciated, and Worthy'. I thought it makes a great acronym. so it's become my LAW. Hilary, our now 95-year-old POM volunteer, has helped me to spread the 'loved and appreciated' message by embroidering it onto aprons and tea towels. I love wearing mine as a reminder to love and appreciate myself and others. Another way I like to spread the love message is to bake cakes in heart-shaped cake pans.

The next chapter offers more ways to be kinder and compassionate, I hope you enjoy.

Six Powerful Ways To Be Kinder and More Compassionate (To Yourself Too!)

Here are six simple ways to incorporate more kindness into our daily lives. Giving ourselves a break and being more friendly to ourselves inspires us to be less harsh on others too.

There is an interrelation between kindness to self and others. As Aesop said, 'No act of kindness, no matter how small, is ever wasted.' [4]

Here are some ways we can practice it:

1. Replace critical self-talk with positive, kind encouragement

Kind, encouraging teachers promote learning, while harsh, critical ones make it difficult for students to learn, so become your own kind encouraging teacher. Kind self-talk can help us be more understanding and compassionate toward others, and it's just as important to offer it to yourself too. Go on, have a kind chat with yourself now!

2. Letting go of high expectations

It's easy to set unrealistic expectations for ourselves and others. Pema Chödrön, in her book *Start Where You Are: A Guide to Compassionate Living*,[5] advises against this. Setting achievable goals and celebrating t hem with kind encouragement motivates us to keep going. When we can't achieve our goals, it's just as important to be *aware* of the potential for our critical inner voice to arise, and to instead, offer ourselves kind, gentle encouragement. This can help us to not hold others to our expectations.

For example, as parents, it's easy to have expectations of what we think our children should do. Letting go of these expectations and allowing them to make their own choices and reach their potential, while still being available to offer encouragement, support and assistance when requested is beneficial to all.

Striving for perfection is an unrealistic expectation too. For me right now, this means not trying to include everything when writing these reflections. When I tune into my wise self, I'm reminded to simply do my best to share what has helped me, and to let go of perfectionism.

3. Release judgment of yourself and others

As shared previously, we are all doing our best with what we know at the time. Show kindness and encouragement to all, including yourself.

4. Approve of and accept yourself

Approve of yourself. Give yourself the validation you need, instead of seeking it externally. We can only recognise others' approval if we first approve of ourselves. Tune into your wise self for kind encouragement like 'I am doing my best, which is pretty awesome'. Remember there are plenty of people who think you are awesome. Yes, you reading this—and me too! And they are not wrong! I've learned that out of 100 people you meet, one-third will like you, one third will feel indifferent and one-third will dislike you. Focus on accepting yourself as you are right now and being the best version of yourself for those who appreciate you for who you are.

5. Respect yourself

Make a commitment to treat yourself as you would want others to treat you—with kindness, respect, love, understanding, and compassion.

6. Value your contributions and recognise the difference you make

Value and be grateful to yourself for all the efforts you make to be 'better for others'—and also be grateful for the opportunities others give you to do so. Spend some time feeling happy about all the ways you are being a kind, encouraging, positive force in the world. There's no need to tie this to career status either. It doesn't matter what we do for work—whether we work in a bakery, sell clothes, or practice medicine, when we approach our work with the intention of connecting with and benefiting others, we can't go wrong.

I once heard of a food services worker who delivered the meals in a cancer hospital. She was, according to the patients she served, administering as good as, if not better medicine than the doctors and professionals involved in their care. She was dispensing and delivering the medicine of kindness, just by being who she was.

When we have a kind 'what can I do for you?' attitude instead of a 'what about me?' mentality, true happiness and meaning are guaranteed, no matter our job.

Now you're on the kindness journey, head to the next chapter for even more ideas on how to further enrich your life with it.

Other Easy Hacks to Be Kinder and More Compassionate

Simplify things

Sometimes, I complicate things unnecessarily. Simplifying tasks, explanations, and life in general is an act of kindness toward myself and others. Breaking tasks into steps, using understandable language, and decluttering our environment brings ease and simplicity to our lives. Decluttering can include a wardrobe overhaul, tidying up the house, or cleaning our desk, this reduces visual clutter, simplifies clothing choices, and frees our minds. We can also simplify our minds by letting go of unnecessary worry, stress, and grudges. Practices like yoga, meditation, and mindfulness can help.

Avoid multitasking

While I used to take pride in my ability to multitask, I now understand it negatively effects my focus. Being mindful of where attention is needed, and committing fully to it is far more effective. To be kinder to myself and others, I make a point of putting away my phone during conversations and giving my attention to eating lunch with my friend, savouring the food, listening and paying attention, being present. With today's distractions, being present with each other is one of the kindest things we can do.

Focus on the feeling rather than the outcome

Rather than focusing on external achievements or end results, focusing instead on the ongoing feeling we want to experience can motivate us. For example:

- Eating healthier and exercising to *feel* good about our bodies and ourselves.
- Practicing patience or meditation to *feel* more relaxed and calm.
- Completing this reflection to *feel* satisfied with having done my best to share what I find useful.
- Befriending negative self-talk to *feel* more compassionate, and confident.
- Doing kind acts to *feel* happy and proud of being a positive, kind force in the world.

Be aware of the temptation to compare yourself to others

When we compare our qualities or lives to others and find lack, we erode our self-confidence. We do this when we focus on what is going wrong, our weaknesses or ways we are not as good as others—this is toxic to our well-being and healthy sense of self. Instead, when we choose to pay attention to what is going right, our unique gifts and strengths and how we can use these to be of benefit to others, our confidence and happiness blooms.

Make and keep realistic commitments

Keeping commitments brings us peace of mind and helps us feel good about ourselves by respecting others. Have you ever felt like giving up on a commitment you've made? I certainly have, for example when I first began writing my weekly blogs to get POM up and running. Many times moments of doubt crept in, and I considered giving up altogether, with thoughts like, 'It's all too hard; I think I will give up.' But I kept going.

Some things that help me make and keep realistic commitments include:

- Only making commitments I intend to keep
- Avoiding over-commitment
- Stocktaking my resources before making a commitment.
- Making sincere commitments but accepting when something unforeseen prevents me from keeping them.

Have realistic expectations of yourself and others

There is a significant difference between expectation and anticipation. Lama Marut teaches that 'expectation is disappointment in training.' Expectation often carries a demanding, controlling quality. In contrast, anticipation is hopeful, looking forward to something positive. Studies show that having something to look forward to with anticipation—rather than expectation—helps create a positive mood and decreases stress. Sri Chinmoy, an Indian spiritual teacher, states, 'Peace begins when expectation ends.' [6]

Sometimes, when I ask for help, I may impose high, unrealistic expectations and demands on others and myself regarding what 'should' be achieved and how. It is much better to ask for what we need from the wise perspective of anticipation rather than expectation.

And sometimes it's the unexpected that can be our kindness reminder. Read on to find out why.

Tripping Over–A Kindness Reminder

A recent trip during a morning run reminded me of the harm in blame and judgment. Embracing kindness, discernment, and self-awareness fosters positive change and honours our diverse experiences.

I remembered how unhelpful it is to blame, judge, or criticise others (and myself) when I tripped while doing a morning plod around the block. It was a rather spectacular stumble, resulting in a lump on my forehead, a graze on my knee, a black eye, and a sprained wrist!

As soon as I hit the concrete, I let out expletives, and my funny mind went to all sorts of unhelpful places. First, I looked for something or someone to blame: the curb, the dog, my sneakers. Then I turned on myself, criticising my clumsiness, rushing, and lack of mindfulness. But was any of this kind, necessary, or helpful? No! I befriended my critical voice with a 'thanks for sharing' and went on to check in for a more helpful habit.

So, what did I need? What was a more helpful habit to replace my tendency to blame and self-criticise? Awareness, tuning into my wise self and kind encouragement were the answers! I stuck a spanner in the blame and criticism habit cog—the spanner of kindness—and it worked instantly. I picked myself up and told myself, 'That can happen, and it did; let's get you home and cleaned up.' I also acknowledged how grateful I was I wasn't wearing my glasses and had done no serious damage.

It was the perfect antidote to wallowing in victimhood; allowing me to cultivate more understanding, responsibility, and positive change.

On judgement and discernment

As I understand it, judgement is when we form an opinion about a person or situation based on the information we *think* we have. The trouble is, we rarely know the full story. Judgement often carries blame towards others or ourselves. In my case, when I met the pavement face first that morning, I immediately judged myself as clumsy and unmindful. But was that really true? One moment of inattention doesn't mean I'm always clumsy or never mindful. By noticing how quickly my mind jumped to blame, I could gently question whether that story was accurate or helpful.

Discernment, however, comes from understanding built through practice in ethics, compassion, and awareness. It's a wiser, kinder way of seeing and helps us respond in ways that actually support us. And the wisest response is almost always kindness. When we pause, we can listen to this wiser part of ourselves and let it guide us with gentle encouragement.

The Dalai Lama words, 'Love is the absence of judgement,' [7] really ups the difference between judgment and discernment.

Buddhist practice leads us to be discerning about 'things to take up' and 'things to give up' in order to be a happier, more positive force in the world. We require discernment to know what habits are helpful and what habits could do with an overhaul.

Some things that help me when I notice this habit of blame and criticism of myself or others is to:

- **Bring a sense of curiosity and awareness to this pattern.** Befriend the unhelpful habit with 'Thanks for sharing,' Oh my funny mind, there it goes criticising and judging again.' I then tune into my wise self to insert a new, more helpful habit of kindness to replace the judging/blaming one.

- **Celebrate diversity.** For example, when I see someone in the street and go to judge their appearance or manner, I try to remember to celebrate that diversity and variety instead of judging them and creating separation.

We all judge a lot in our minds, but how can we be discerning about whether to communicate this? I find it helpful to recall Rumi's wisdom: 'Before you speak, let your word pass through three gates. Is it true? Is it necessary? Is it kind?' [8] Here's to laying out the welcome mat for that approach!

And how about laying out a welcome mat for dragons at the same time? What am I talking about? Join me in the final chapter to find out.

Befriending Dragons

During a Chinese New Year yoga retreat, I learned to listen to my wise self for some kind encouragement. By befriending my inner dragons, fears transformed into opportunities for growth.

I learned a valuable lesson about listening to my wise, intuitive self and befriending dragons during a Chinese New Year yoga retreat led by the fabulous, fun, and unconventional yoga teacher Andrew Mournehis. For the past twenty years during Chinese New Year, this retreat has incorporated mythology, yoga asanas, and vision board creation for the year ahead.

I used to think retreats sounded wonderfully relaxing, with pampering and time to restore. While retreats can be like this, the ones I've attended have offered more than just relaxation—they have provided remarkable opportunities to confront and learn from unhelpful habits and beliefs. So, I often find the idea of going on retreat somewhat daunting, knowing it will involve internal challenges, but I always end up appreciating this opportunity for growth.

My daughter enthusiastically joined me for the retreat, but as an introvert (though I've become more content and comfortable with this aspect of myself), I was daunted by some of the planned activities such as speaking in a group, dressing up in costumes, and dancing. The organisers asked us to bring gold and red clothing and scarves for the Saturday night celebration. I found a yellow chicken dress and wings, along with red pants and a scarf, planning for my daughter to wear the chicken costume while I wore the pants and scarf. Perfect!

We arrived at the retreat and settled into the beautiful, peaceful surroundings. After an asana class and healthy breakfast of fruit, cereal and sourdough toast, on the Saturday we joined the opening circle, sharing our hopes for the year ahead. I mentioned wanting to face some fears and limiting beliefs, while another participant expressed a desire to slay her fears and demons. I realised that rather than trying to slay my inner fears (soon to be labeled dragons) I wanted to befriend them.

I love the word 'befriend' because it implies accepting the perception of a dragon, fear, or something unwanted, with the willingness to make friends with it. When we can Accept, welcome, and befriend these aspects rather than trying to push away or suppress them, we transform fear, to love. Jalaluddin Rumi's poem, *The Guest House*, beautifully expresses this approach, likening being human to a guest house that hosts many arrivals—sadness, joy, and malice among them. Rumi advises us to welcome and entertain them all—as they may come to clear out space for something new, something we could be grateful for.

Having decided that befriending dragons would be my theme for the retreat, I was on the lookout for my first dragon to meet. It appeared on Saturday evening when we were instructed to gather on the lawn in our yellow and red clothes. My daughter and I went to get ready. I expected to be inconspicuous in my red pants and scarf, letting her shine in the chicken costume. However, she had different ideas, refusing to dress as poultry. Enter my first dragon: the fear of making a fool of myself.

Anxiety washed over me as I wondered where this unhelpful habit originated, perhaps some traumatic childhood event. I felt tempted to invent a headache or find any excuse to avoid the event, but knew this wasn't the best approach.

Instead, I used my ABCD practice: I accepted the anxiety and fear, breathed through the feeling without suppression or feeding it, allowing it to pass through. By befriending the fear and critical thoughts and thanking them for sharing, it freed me to check in with my wise self, who kindly encouraged and reassured me I could wear the costume and have fun.

We joined the others on the lawn, and they were beaming at me. I, the most introverted person in the most extroverted costume, was by far the most 'out there' as a yellow chicken! I had befriended my dragon fear and was doing okay, I even felt reasonably relaxed!

The next dragon flew in when we were asked to form two lines and dance down the middle to Diana Ross' *I'm Coming Out* [9] anthem. As my turn approached, anxiety and fear rose again. An invocation of the ABCD though meant I could dance through the crowd, even using my chicken wings as fans for effect. It was liberating to befriend the fear and embrace the fun.

Later, a friend asked if I was the chicken in the photo on Andrew's Facebook page. 'Yes, that was me,' I replied, feeling no fear about being 'exposed' as I'd already befriended my 'make a fool of myself' dragon. As Rumi's poem suggests, welcoming and befriending the unwanted guest or dragon, allows for uplifting gratitude and the release of fear.

I was thrilled I'd listened to the kind, encouraging best friend on my left shoulder telling me, 'We've got this'. That voice and the one that befriended my critical taskmaster who was so worried I'd make a fool of myself, launched me out of my comfort zone and into the fun zone.

HEART-FRIENDLY WAYS TO PRACTICE

Given that this is the final reflection in this Section, and the book please join me in rejoicing in the fact that we and others have read, contemplated or practiced the practices and reflections in this section on kindness and throughout the whole book to foster our understanding of how to live a good life.

You may like to:

- Having looked at ways we can practice kindness, make a list of ways you can be kinder both to yourself and to others.
- Think of someone who has shown you kindness and reflect on how their kindness has impacted you and your life.
- Contemplate ways you can change your negative perception into a more positive outlook.
- Consider how implementing a kind boundary may prevent harm and how to do this.
- Think about ways you can be a kind, encouraging friend to yourself. Write down your own list of kind, encouraging slogans to say to yourself in times of need.

- Be aware of the critical self-talk happening on your right shoulder and tune in to listen to the wise encouraging voice on the left. You may want to write down some of your critical thoughts and their kind encouraging antidotes.

The Evening Loll

We outlined a morning gratitude practice called 'The Morning Loll' in Section 1: Gratitude, on pg 15.

To finish off, here is an 'Evening Loll':

- When you go to bed, recall all the ways you were a kind, positive force in the world during your day.

- Feel really happy about what you've done and dedicate this positive energy to the health and well-being of everyone, including yourself.

- You can also recall the kindness of others.

- I find this a great way to peacefully go to sleep. You may, too.

Let's feel glad for all the positive energy we have created together and dedicate this to the happiness and wellbeing of all.

My Religion is Kindness

1. Dalai Lama, *Brainy Quotes*: https://www.brainyquote.com/quotes/dalai_lama_108820

Kindness can have a profound, lasting effect

2. Robert Ingersoll, *The Random Acts of Kindness Site*: https://www.randomactsofkindness.org

Do your best, until you know better

3. Maya Angelou, *Goodreads Quotes, The Goodreads Site*: https://www.goodreads.com/quotes/7273813-do-the-best-you-can-until-you-know-better-then#:~:text=Sign%20Up%20Now

Ways to be kinder and more compassionate

4. Aesop, *Brainly Quotes, The Brainy Quotes Site*: https://www.brainyquote.com/quotes/aesop_109734

5. Pema Chödrön, *When Things Fall Apart: Heart Advices For Difficult Times*, (Boston Shambhala, 2002).

Peace begins when expectation ends

6. Sri Chinmoy, *Sri Chinmoy Library Site*: https://www.srichinmoylibrary.com/scm-9

Love is the absence of judgement

7. Dalai Lama, *Goodreads Quotes, The Goodreads Site:* https://www.goodreads.com/quotes/11807-love-is-the-absence-of-judgment

8. Rumi, Jalai Al-Din, Rumi, *Goodreads Quotes, The Goodreads Site*: https://www.goodreads.com/quotes/7852322-before-you-speak-let-your-words-pass-through-three-gates

9. Dianna Ross – *I'm Coming Out* - https://www.youtube.com/watch?v=6CHdKORwPEQ

EPILOGUE

Way back in the introduction I described how, at five years old, feeling scared and sad, a quiet spark of knowing flickered to light—a sense that I was not alone, not separate.

That loving, comforting, reassuring presence within was later rekindled through my interest in spirituality and fanned by the wise and generous people I have thankfully learned from. Even more recently, it ignited the drive in me to share through this book.

Thank you for reading, and for spending your time exploring these ideas and practices with me. Together we've explored a collection of heartfelt ingredients and tools and played with ways to homebake a happy meaningful life—complete with a few baking flops, AKA 'learning experiences', along the way.

It is my warmest wish that you have fun with your own homebaking too, using some of the ingredients and tools from this book to connect with your innate, intuitive wise self and to discover love, belonging, forgiveness, meaning, and a true expression of wonderful you. Just keep cooking I say!

When we remember to connect to, listen and take action from that wisdom and be an encouraging best friend to ourselves, the joy bubbles forth.

I hope you can take these homebaked, tested and tried wisdoms with you and enjoy the process—skipping when you can, tripping when you must, and learning all the while. And when your wise director invites you to bake even more kindness into your life, my other book: *Skipping and Tripping along the Kindness Path* will be there for you.

APPENDIX

Full Meditation Version of Tong Len

Before engaging in a meditation like Tong Len, it's helpful to do some meditation preliminaries that help us feel present and relaxed. These are presented in the Section 6, 'Defrazzling: Coming Back to the Present' on page 160

Then we are ready to practice Tong Len.

1. Bring to mind someone who is suffering.

This can be a person you know, a group of people you are aware of, or a version of yourself going through a hard time. Clarify the nature of their particular suffering– maybe they are sick, sad, worried, in an unsafe situation, facing great hardship through conflict, financial difficulties, or disaster. Perhaps they are lonely, confused, or grieving.

2. Picture the person (or group) sitting in front of you.

Visualise their suffering as a dark cloud around their hearts. Use the power of your in-breath to imagine concentrating this cloud of suffering into a smaller mass until it is the size of a small pea. Continue to use the inbreath to draw it up from their heart and through their body, and out through their nostril.

Imagine it settles and hovers as a small concentrated pea-sized ball of suffering between you and them.

If you are working with a group of people, you may want to visualise one representative person in front of the others and concentrate on this specific person. You could also visualise a version of yourself in front of you, and do this meditation for that suffering version of you.

3. Destroy the Suffering

We can do this in one of two ways, depending on how comfortable we feel about taking suffering into our own bodies—especially when we are new to this meditation, we can feel understandably apprehensive about that. What matters is our intention to transform suffering into peace, so here are two options for doing that:

a. Continue to use the in-breath to take the suffering ball in through your nostril and down to our heart. Visualise the energy of love at your heart destroying it completely, leaving not a trace behind.

b. If you don't feel comfortable taking the suffering into your own body, simply send a beam of love out from your heart to destroy the ball of suffering that's hovering between you.

Either way, it is important to have the conviction that the suffering is completely destroyed.

4. Send love and happiness

Having completely eradicated the suffering, visualise rays of love emanating from your heart. Using the power of the out-breath, feel these rays striking the heart of the person in front of you. Imagine these rays of love carrying anything that person could possibly need:

- Material things like food, water, medicine, shelter, money, or anything else necessary for their comfort.
- Spiritual gifts like contentment and peace of mind, wisdom and clarity about their situation or the courage to change.

You can have fun with this and send them anything in abundance that you feel would make them happy—send the wish for them to feel safe, peaceful, loved, clear-minded, free of pain and sickness, and supported. Visualise these gifts being received by them, thereby granting them relief and true happiness.

5. Rejoice in their happiness.

Spend a moment imagining their suffering is completely relieved and happiness, love and kindness imbues them. See them as content and at peace. Now you are ready to farewell them by gradually allowing their image to fade from your mind

6. Bask in the positive energy

Allow yourself to feel the goodness of engaging in this meditation to nurture compassion for both others and yourself. Share the positive energy you have cultivated through this meditation for the benefit of everyone's health and well-being.

7. Return to the present

Recenter your focus on the present moment, bring your awareness back to the room, and reconnect with your breath. Give a gentle wiggle to your fingers and toes, then slowly begin to open your eyes.

Although this is all visualised in the mind, in my experience, it has influenced feeling and actions of love, kindness and compassion in my daily life.

ABOUT THE AUTHOR

Maree Allan Fowler is a yoga teacher, aged care worker and the founder of POM (Peace of Mind – Melbourne), a small cottage-industry initiative that raises funds for education projects both here in Australia and overseas.

She is qualified as an occupational therapist and primary school teacher and has worked as a Buddhist educator in primary schools. Maree has also taught Tibetan Buddhism and yoga philosophy to adult students in Melbourne. She volunteers in community mental health and at the Asylum Seeker Resource Centre.

Maree lives in Melbourne with her husband, E, and is the mother of four adult children.

www.ingramcontent.com/pod-product-compliance
Ingram Content Group UK Ltd.
Pitfield, Milton Keynes, MK11 3LW, UK
UKHW042007190726
13854UKWH00005B/2200

9 781764 225205